a shift to love

a shift to love

ZEN STORIES AND LESSONS
BY ALEX MILL

Zen Life Books

Zen Life Books
782 Trail Ridge Drive
Louisville, CO 80027
www.zenlifebooks.com

Copyright © 2018 by Alex Mill
Edited by Sara Stibitz

First Edition

ISBN-13: 978-0-578-42420-0
ISBN-10: 0-578-42420-7

To Mom and Dad

You may not have always understood what I did or why I did it, but you always supported me without fail. Thank you for being my first teachers in unconditional love.
I love you.

CONTENTS

PREFACE

After training in a Zen monastery for nearly 14 years, I discovered that people were extremely curious to hear about my experiences. They would ask me, "What was it like? What inspired you to go? What did you learn? Why did you leave?"

As I began to share my stories with readers, audiences, retreatants, and clients, I realized they were really curious about how they could incorporate the teachings and the wisdom I learned into their own lives. Without going to a distant monastery for years on end, how could they too benefit from what I had experienced? I quickly saw that the practices and perspectives I learned were not only helpful to monks, but they were also beneficial to lay people out in the world. We were all looking to find our way amidst the same inner dilemmas and challenges. It's just that outside the monastery, there was much more confusion about what the cause of those were and less support to turn them around.

We as human beings have a very interesting spiritual opportunity here on this planet. We have been given the choice between living in a delusion or living in Life. Part of why this book exists is because I see that distinction extremely clearly. I see what people are up against. A force inside of every one of us looks outward and thinks the change needs to happen "out there." And so we play the captivating (but frustrating) shell game to see how we can rearrange the world, others, and ourselves in order to be harmonious. We're caught in this ongoing manipulation of superficial circumstances in order to make lasting change. But this, unfortunately, will never happen. The very system driving this approach is what's keeping it going.

I wrote these stories as my glorious opportunity and duty. This book was my way of giving back what I had been so generously given. I chose the format of "stories and lessons" because I have found they are the most captivating way to share deep principles that go straight to the heart.

Stories have a way of bypassing the intellect striving to understand. A story helps a person's brain relax and intuitively understand how the teachings relate to them from *the inside*, rather than something coming at them from *the outside*. Most of the great spiritual teachings have come to us this way for this purpose. There's no resistance to a story as there is to a directive.

The chapters in this book are not rules. They are not even suggestions for ways to change. They are merely gateways for you to see something differently. They encourage you to let go and see how what you read applies in your own experience.

They are also written as individual passages that stand alone as well as relate to the whole. Please feel free to begin at the beginning or read a random chapter by your night table when you get up in the morning. Many themes repeat because sometimes a different example is needed to illustrate a point. I've made it no secret that one of my favorite books is *Zen Flesh, Zen Bones* by Paul Reps and Nyogen Senzaki. Their collection "101 Zen Stories" continues to inspire my own writing to fulfill the role of "modern day Zen stories," or as I subtitled my previous book, *Spiritual Training for Modern Times*.

This book is not a self-improvement book. There is no self to improve. You are encouraged to read and look inward. To see what there is for you to see. If you think you understand something or "get it," note how that happened and let it go. Consider that comprehension isn't the point of this book. In fact, the more you claim to understand, the less you really do. Such is the irony of Zen.

This book is a limitation. Most of the great masters have claimed that words won't help. Lao Tzu said, *"The Tao that can be told is not the eternal Tao."*

So what then?

My fourth book, this book you hold in your hands, *A Shift to Love: Zen Stories and Lessons by Alex Mill,* is my fourth attempt to inspire you to take action. While it may be tempting for you to "know more," understand that your *experience* is all that matters. I love the expression, "You'll never learn how to ride a bike from a book." If the stories and lessons in this book speak to you, if they call to you to go deeper into yourself, my encouragement is to follow that calling. Avail yourself of that proverbial "bike," get on it, and experience it for yourself.

As your teacher and guide throughout this book, I will share ways for you to do that.

In lovingkindness,

Alex

INTRODUCTION

Enlightenment is an accident.
Practice makes us accident-prone.
—Zen Saying

I t happens in an instant.

One moment you see life in a particular way and then in a flash, it's completely different.

I'm sure you can recall a time when this happened in your life. A time when your world was blown open. Or blown down.

When I was a young child, I was in love with playing outdoors. My backyard opened up to a vast forest where I would spend hours imagining I was a swashbuckler forging new lands, conquering monsters, and initiating exciting adventures. A simple branch was my sword and the random debris in the woods became the spaceships, enemies, and treasure I would encounter along the way. It was sheer magic!

Until one day I came back home from school and decided to revisit my mighty forest playground. As I approached it, I remember being disappointed by how small it really was. Had it always been like this? Once inside, there was nothing too terribly fun about it either. The brambles cut my ankles. The bugs were annoying. And I was at an awkward loss as to what I was supposed to be doing there now that I was standing in the middle of it.

Momentarily rescuing me from my discomfort, I suddenly remembered a special tree that I loved. I went over to go see if it was still there. Sure enough, it was! It was an unusual tree that looked as if it had grown a couple feet up out of the ground and then decided to make a right angle turn sideways, parallel to the forest floor for several yards. It was perfect for hoisting myself up onto it, dangling my feet over the edge, and surveying the land around me. But sitting up there now created this empty feeling inside. There was nothing to see. It wasn't that high. And it was just – b o r i n g.

I was suffering from a terminal illness that I would later refer to as "having become a grown up."

It was as if magic was replaced with blah, and wonder transformed into something wrong and not enough.

I look back on that day as a turning point – a clear departure from my innocence of youth and the onset of the conditioned reality of being an adult. Never to return.

a shift to love

I didn't realize it at the time, but my discovery of Zen many years later at the age of 29 was going to become my journey back in time. I was going to find what I had lost in that forest. I was going to reunite with that bright-eyed boy who was out there waiting for me. Who needed me and who never lost hope.

It wasn't going to be easy because instead of serpents, aliens, and King Kong between us, I was going to face the inner voices that would try to thwart me at every turn. I had to pull out some major willpower to forge past these shady characters. It took practice and over a decade of training in a Zen monastery to help me find what I was looking for.

But do you know what I discovered?

In a flash, just as my magical forest was taken from me, a sudden insight and a turn of my attention to compassion miraculously popped my world open and gave it back to me again.

I found this path was not a path at all.

It wasn't as if enlightenment was floating out there on a mountaintop far away. And it wasn't like these voices could actually harm me, either. Everything I needed was right here, right now, always with me, all the time.

The realization of this happened in an instant – with a shift of my attention.

It made me recall the ending of the movie, *The Wizard of Oz*. Do you remember it? It's when Dorothy tapped her ruby slippers together three times, repeated "There's no place like home," and miraculously woke up in her bed in Kansas. She discovered she'd been asleep all along. Her entire journey to and from Oz was just a dream.

That's what the dream of conditioned mind is like too. When you are asleep and dreaming, you need only to open your eyes and wake up. You don't have to trek back from being lost over the rainbow to be in the present. When you are stuck in the drama, you can simply redirect your attention and...poof! You're home again. Instantly.

In this book, I will share personal stories and lessons from my Zen training about how this shift works. I will show you the obstacles you will face along the way, the choices you will need to make, and the possibilities you can create if you commit to making your own shifts to love.

AUTHOR'S NOTE

Chapter titles followed by an asterisk (*) indicate that a version of this chapter was excerpted from my book, *Meditation and Reinventing Yourself.*

Chapter titles followed by a dagger (†) indicate that a version of this chapter was excerpted from my book, *The Zen Life: Spiritual Training for Modern Times.*

Directing your attention
out of the stories
and into Life
is the ultimate
shift to love.

REAL ADVICE

Many people read what I share about my experiences at the Zen monastery and ask for my advice. They want to know what I suggest they do about their relationships, their weight loss journey, their struggle with their boss, their children, and themselves. They want to know how to stop the crazy negative thoughts and how to find self-love despite their faults.

I read posts on social media forums filled with advice. Tips, tricks, articles, case studies, and personal stories. From my own experience, I know how tempting it is to constantly read, listen to and watch inspirational content. It can be very uplifting and illuminating. In fact, when I first found Zen, I obsessively bought every book about Zen I could find because I was addicted to this feeling they produced.

However, I noticed I was doing something rather odd. I was skipping all the exercises in the books and I was avoiding doing the one thing all of them said to do: Meditate. After my ninth book, I realized it was crazy to be reading all these books about meditation and yet not meditate. So I broke down and bought myself a cushion.

And I began to meditate.

That's when things started to change. Things began to slow down. I became more patient, kind, and loving. My girlfriend noticed I was acting differently, and so did all of my friends. I changed.

Had I not stopped to meditate, I'm convinced all those inspirational books would have integrated into my vast library and nothing different would have happened with my life. I would not have sold all of my belongings and traveled cross-country in the direction of the Zen monastery. I would not have decided to visit, train, or practice Zen for over a decade. No transformation would have happened.

Now that I'm out of the monastery coaching clients, helping students, and interacting with people who want to develop personally, professionally, and spiritually, I see them struggling with the same struggles that I did all those years ago. They're reading books, watching videos, liking inspirational quotes, listening to talks and consuming lots of content. They're fascinated by their mental understandings but struggling to wrap their lives around what they're learning.

Within myself, I feel the temptation to want to offer "my answers" to help them. To add to the noise coming at them.

But I know that wouldn't be of true service.

The Korean Zen Master, Seung Sahn, said it best:

Zen means that if you want to understand what a watermelon is, you take a watermelon, get a knife, and cut the watermelon. Then you put a slice into your mouth – boom! Your experience! Words and speech and books and learning cannot deliver this point. Even if you read one hundred books about watermelons, and hear one hundred lectures, they cannot teach as well as one single bite.

So if you want to know my advice, it's not going to be about whether you should leave your partner or stay with him. I won't argue about the benefits of working harder versus being more kind. I won't answer your questions about which books to read about spirituality.

I'm going to suggest you go find out.

I'm going to suggest you sit down on your meditation cushion and sit through the resistance. I'm going to suggest you take that course on self-compassion and experience what a deep, powerful relationship with yourself can be like. I'm going to suggest you get up, shut the book, the computer or the phone off and talk to someone. Listen to them. Sit in silence. Look inside. Ask yourself interested questions.

Don't be like that person Saint Augustine mentions in this quote attributed to him:

Men go abroad to wonder at the heights of mountains, at the huge waves of the sea, at the long courses of the rivers, at the vast com-

pass of the ocean, at the circular motions of the stars, and they pass by themselves without wondering.

Stay with yourself and go as far inward as you can go. Don't play the game of "find the right answer" on the surface of life. Stop rearranging the deck chairs on your Titanic.

Go deeper still and get to the foundation.

Digging tiny potholes all over your yard will not produce water. Staying in one spot and going deep is where your treasure lies. It's where the water will spring forth.

MY DECISIONLESS DECISION

I didn't decide to train in a Zen monastery.

I didn't say to myself one day, "I think I'd like to give up everything I have and go train as a monk in a Zen monastery for 14 years."

Before I discovered Zen, I had no interest in anything even remotely resembling spirituality. I was interested in the exact opposite. I was just a regular artist dude who liked to read a lot and collect shiny objects. By all rights, I had everything I thought I should have that would warrant happiness. My planets had aligned. I had the magnificent home, the beautiful girlfriend, the excellent job, the money to buy whatever I wanted, the free time to do my artwork, and all the friends I could ever want.

So, on that summer day in 1999 when I followed my girlfriend into that new age bookstore on South Street, it was merely to humor her. On my own, I would never have been caught dead in there. I often scoffed about how it was the "$500 Self-Help

Buddha Statue Shop," a store full of expensive junk to buy that signaled to everyone you were enlightened because you owned it.

But that weekend, my girlfriend's best friend from out of town came to visit, and they both wanted to go in and look around, so I joined them. Being the good boyfriend, I left them to wander about together, and while they did I tried to keep my mouth shut and stay out of trouble.

I picked up a random book off the tabletop that caught my eye. It had a long, weird title and a drawing on the cover of something – I didn't know what. As I thumbed through this slim book, I noticed the text inside was handwritten and there were cute drawings scattered throughout. I looked at the back cover and there was a photo of the author, and she looked radiant. Beaming.

Now, I've got to tell you that everything about this book should have sent me a strong signal to put it down and avoid it at all costs. Because serious authors wrote the books I was interested in. Serious authors with serious photos of them taken in shadows with serious looks on their faces. They weren't cutesie. They were authors like Edgar Allen Poe. Grim and menacing.

But for whatever unknown reason, I started to read this book. And from the first few words in, I was hooked. The author was talking about life as though she was talking about my life. And the life and thoughts were my life and thoughts. She was describing me and what I was struggling with, even though I would never have said I was struggling. It was as if she was standing in my head speaking through me explaining why I experienced life the way I did.

One passage in particular jumped out at me. Here's my paraphrase of it:

One process does not lead to another. One process leads to more of that process. So wanting does not equal having. Only having equals having. Just as wanting only leads to more wanting. If I wanted to experience having – I needed to have, not want. The same was true with peace. If I wanted peace, I needed to experience peace. I was not going to have peace by striving after peace.

I saw my life flash before my eyes. The insight was so simple, yet so profound. Suddenly everything made sense.

Even though I was not miserable, I wasn't exactly happy. I would describe my life as a series of "seeking moments" that led to briefly obtaining what I was seeking. And those only resulted in me seeking again, like I was some bottomless hole that could never be filled. There were always going to be new things to have, new places to see, new people to meet, and new experiences, which in itself could be okay. The trouble was that I never felt like I was there with any of them. While I was obtaining one, I was thinking about how I could get the other. I never had anything. I was eternally wanting. In the process, I was missing out on my life and feeding my dissatisfaction instead.

My girlfriend passed me while I was reading this book several times and finally said, "It looks like you're enjoying this book. If you like it so much, you should just buy it." So I did.

Then in a couple of days, I bought another. And another. I became addicted to these "Zen books."

However, nothing would have ever changed in my life had I not done one simple thing. Meditate.

I almost didn't. You see, these books were full of exercises to do, and there were constant encouragements to meditate. I just gleefully skipped those. They interrupted the flow of my reading. And what I was reading was so inspiring.

Stop to do an exercise? Nah, I don't think so.

It was by the ninth book that it finally dawned on me: How ridiculous to be buying and reading books about meditation and not be meditating.

That afternoon, before work, I went to that same "$500 Self-Help Buddha Statue Shop" and bought myself a meditation cushion.

That's when everything changed for me.

That's when I saw how I was living my life. I saw what wasn't working. I saw how I was living as a collector who was never satisfied.

Of course, I thought, if the answer wasn't in what I purchased or owned then the answer must be "not to purchase or own" anything. For a while, I tried to stop myself from buying anything. I got rid of a bunch of stuff. But I wasn't any happier. I understood the concepts, but conditioned mind was concluding what to do with my understanding and messing things up. It took me a while to realize this wasn't the answer – that's just the other side of the duality.

Around the same time, my girlfriend announced that she wanted us to travel cross-country together. It was a perfect opportunity to visit a Zen monastery that would be at the end of our trip in California. I said nothing but kept it in my mind for when the time came to discuss it with her.

In the process of preparing for this trip, I sold most of my belongings. It was incredibly challenging. I had *lots* of fantastic stuff. Art books worth a great deal. Hundreds of compact discs. The used bookstores and record shops thought I was nuts for parting with such collectible stuff. But I needed the money to fund our trip. Besides, I had found Zen and I no longer needed these things.

I said this on the outside while my stomach did flip-flops on the inside. Everything I was doing was threatening my identity and it felt horrible.

So off we went across the country.

I remember casually telling my girlfriend that I thought it would be fun to visit a Zen monastery when we arrived in California. She agreed. When we got to Tennessee, I called the monastery to see if we could arrange a visit. I got a jovial woman on the phone who said, "Of course" and then told me she would send me an email that would include all the information I needed about the orientation. I was excited.

However, when we got to Mississippi, things took a drastic turn.

We went to visit a friend of mine. She had spent years in an Ashram training in spirituality, meditation, and yoga. She and I connected that year and along the way she became a bit of a spiritual mentor to me, although I would never have called her that. She was always just Fruma to me.

When I spoke to her, I had told her a few stories about how I was struggling with my girlfriend, and she would give me straight-forward advice.

Rather blunt advice. Advice that left me inspired yet slightly disturbed.

For example, she once told me "The world wants an honest Alex, not a nice Alex." That simple sentence floated around in my head for a long time, and after a while, I suddenly grasped what she meant. I was having trouble saying "no" to my girlfriend and instead did some rather foolish things to please her. I wasn't telling her what I wanted and this was making me upset. "Of course," I thought, "the world needs an honest Alex who will speak the truth instead of a nice Alex who will simply do what will please others."

So when I saw Fruma in Mississippi and we had some time alone together, she pulled no punches and said, "What are you doing on this stupid trip with this stupid girl?"

My heart made a familiar Fruma thud. Did she just say what I thought she said? I sat in silence for a bit because I didn't know what to say.

Finally, I knew she was reading my mind. I *did* think this trip was stupid and I did see my girlfriend as this silly girl who was in control of me. Again. Somehow, I had been talked into yet another ridiculous situation that had more to do with me pleasing her rather than staying true to myself. And it was costing *me* money and going to leave us in a bad way in the end.

I told Fruma she was right. But what to do? Then she asked me, "If you weren't on this stupid trip with this stupid girl, what would you be doing?"

Without any hesitation at all, I said, "I'd be in a monastery."

Now we both sat in silence for a bit to let that sink in. Finally, she said, "That's not a typical response from a man your age, so I suggest you meditate on this a bit."

But at that moment, it became clear that I wanted to see if it would be possible to extend my visit to the Zen monastery.

Later that night, I told my girlfriend that I'd like to see if I could stay there a month. She was a little hesitant, but she had been very supportive of me the whole time. She saw how powerful meditation and the practice I was doing in those books were for me. The moment I began meditating I became more loving, kind, and attentive. She said yes.

I called the monastery to discuss the possibility. I remember getting the same jovial woman on the phone again. She agreed on the more extended stay but said that I would need to get a few other details taken care of to proceed. For example, because of the longer time commitment, I would need to have a tetanus shot. I remember agreeing because I was excited my request was granted so quickly (I later found out that "the jovial woman" was to be my future Zen teacher).

As I got my other details in order, and the reality of me parting from my girlfriend for a month started to settle in, I became uneasy. This decision, while exciting, began tugging at my heartstrings. My girlfriend started calling herself "The Lone Wolf," and she made this crayon drawing of herself at sea with me far away on some distant shore. It made me cry to look at it.

In San Diego, I got my tetanus shot and began my half-day bus trip up north to the monastery. I had my "hobo" sleeping bag packed up with minimal belongings and tears in my eyes, sobbing goodbye to my girlfriend. I think the last thing I said to her before boarding the bus was, "You're the best girlfriend in the world."

Pulling away from that bus station was hard. The same flip-flop in my stomach started to happen as I realized everything familiar to me was getting further and further away. My girlfriend took the van, our cell phone, our money and everything we owned to settle in California for a short while. I had next to nothing and I was going off to God-knows-where.

When I was finally dropped off at the last Greyhound bus station, I was exhausted. My trip began early in the morning and now it was late in the afternoon, approaching evening. I was supposed to meet a monk at the bus station who was going to pick me up. I had no way to contact anyone. No one at the nearly abandoned station looked like a monk.

What did a monk look like anyway?

I waited and waited for over 20 minutes. Finally, a young woman pulled up in a station wagon and began looking around. She was wearing beads around her neck, and when our eyes met, she asked, "Alex?"

I sighed in relief and smiled. She looked down at my hobo bag to see if she could help me load up for the ride to the monastery, but I had it under control. The expression on her face led me to believe that no one else showed up like a homeless person to go to the monastery.

Our car ride was in silence, as per the guidelines, so all I could do was sit there with the endless stream of thoughts racing through my head. The highways turned into four-lane roads, which turned into two-lane roads, which wound deeper and deeper into the woods. The weather got more drastic. Eternally sunny San Diego seemed like a distant dream as the cold, windy rain dropped in bucket loads onto our windshield. The sound of the wipers quickly swooshing mirrored the racing of my heart.

After a couple more hours of traveling, the winding road turned into a narrow dirt road that ran up alongside a hill. I could barely see anything because it was so dark.

We finally slowed down and passed a single cattle gate. The monk stepped out of the car quickly to close it behind us and then got back in out of the rain. We crawled at five mph along our final stretch. I saw some lights up ahead in windows to a building on the hill we passed and then more darkness.

She parked before a small brown trailer sitting in the woods. Together we walked inside and she showed me the contents with her flashlight.

"This is your hermitage." She said with her voice slightly raised so it could be heard over the rain. "Here's the propane tank for your heater." On top of the tank was a short metal neck attached to a small round grill. "Here's how to light it. Be sure *not* to keep it on overnight. The fumes are toxic and if you leave it lit while you sleep, you might not wake up." She said this in a way that was supposed to be funny. But after an entire day's worth of travel and the shock that had set into my system, I just nodded while she laughed awkwardly to herself.

Before she left, she asked if I had a flashlight. I said yes and pulled mine out from the hobo bag. She said, "If you'd like to join us for meditation and then something to eat, the hall is back where we passed." I thanked her, and she left.

There was no electricity in my "hermitage." Just an oil lamp in the corner by the mattress on a plywood box. It was a good thing I wasn't claustrophobic because there was no room in this structure for more than me and my bag.

I went over to the lamp and attempted to light it. I noticed the box of matches sitting by it was damp and so I had to strike the box repeatedly. After the ninth attempt, panic began to set in as my strikes became more and more frantic. I finally put the box down as I thought I was about to lose it.

Flashes of my girlfriend by herself in a strange place, The Lone Wolf, me in the dark, in hell with this wet box, the futility of me trying to light a godforsaken match, paper ripping from the box, my breath showing in the flashlight beam, the sound of rain crashing on all sides, buried alive, my heart racing, and feeling desperately alone. Panic!

Finally, I remembered to drop everything and focus on my breath.

A life raft.

I began to breathe consciously. Just like I had been doing since the moment I started meditating. The way I had been meditating in the van as I traveled cross-country. The way I had been training myself to redirect my attention, shifting my focus from my thoughts to my breath, again and again.

I felt myself instantly calm down. I picked up the box, struck it with another match, and it immediately lit. The oil lamp glowed warmly and illuminated the hermitage.

My new home.

I plopped down on the bed and continued to focus on my breath and listen to the rainfall.

There was nothing left to do but undo my sleeping bag, prepare to join meditation, and get something to eat. I was exhausted.

That was Day 1.

WITHOUT MISSING A BEAT

Several weeks after I arrived at the monastery, I pulled a note off the message board informing me that I would be participating in the upcoming retreat. It said that I would be taking the role of a retreatant and the only working meditation I was expected to do for the entire week was to help out in the kitchen with dishes. Oh, and it was starting tonight!

From the moment I entered that retreat until it finished, I was in a whirl. I laughed, I cried, I broke down to pieces, and rose back up stronger than before. I had never imagined the practice I was doing was as deep and as transformative as it was. This was more than just sitting down on a meditation cushion, facing a blank wall, and becoming mindful. It asked me to go to the core of what it meant to be a human being. I was led to traverse the challenging minefield of emotions, thoughts, habits, and unhelpful behaviors to ultimately find who I authentically was when all of it was stripped away.

What struck me most was the compassion and presence of my facilitator. Outside the retreat, Mary was the current Work Director. Seeing her dressed up completely in black to guide us in this retreat took me aback since she was typically wearing jean overalls and flannel shirts. Her entire demeanor was different, too. She gently navigated the room with all of us and was constantly aware of the energy we were bringing. She decided when to allow us to explore and share and when to wrangle us in. We were all process-ing some very deep, personal stories and exposing some tough, inner demons in that room. The skill she employed to contend with them was awe-inspiring.

It was, however, the ceremony at the end that blew my mind. It was simply breathtaking. It was as though Mary was conducting a Buddhist exorcism on us – driving the demons out and inviting compassion in instead. I'd never experienced anything like it before in my entire life. The calm I felt once the torrent of tears subsided left my heart floating and my mind grounded.

When my processing was complete, I looked into Mary's eyes and was met by her gentleness. She smiled and checked in to see if I was truly ready to leave the circle. I nodded and we finished up with our hands on our hearts, eyes closed, facing a blank wall, and silently speaking words of compassion to ourselves.

After lunch, the retreat was officially over. All of the retreatants were scurrying about getting themselves ready to leave. They had books they'd bought under their arms and luggage rolling along on the porch. Some were being driven to the airport and others were leaving in their own vehicles. I watched as the cars were slowly crawling up the dirt road, over the hill, and around the bend to the outside world. I was acutely aware of the fact that I was staying behind.

Part of me was relieved to have had the sanctuary of the monastery to continue supporting me with this huge opening it created. It was amazing how much energy I had in my body. However, part of me wished I was heading out to see my loved ones alongside everyone else. We all got to know each other intimately and it was sad to see these beautiful people leaving. Especially since I knew that I would likely never see them again. Anonymously they came in and anonymously they left without a trace.

I headed into the kitchen and washed the dishes alongside the monks. I had renewed vigor. Were they always this beautiful? I felt like I was one big, breathing, smiling heart weaving in and out of the kitchen that afternoon.

Coming to the message board after meditation, I pulled a note addressed to me. It read that I was going to be on the tree-clearing crew with the Work Director. A smile broke over my face and I rushed off to get dressed into my work clothes.

There she was, my facilitator, no longer regal but dressed in the grubby work duds I was so used to seeing her in. An enormous pine tree had fallen across the road leading to one of the hermitages and she was up on top of it, wielding her chainsaw like a Jedi knight alongside a couple other monks with chainsaws going. When she saw me approach, she shut her saw off and instructed me to stay clear of the crew. She told me to drag the fallen branches toward the truck only when it was safe to come through. Then she started up her saw, leapt onto the tree, and continued to swipe through the branches and limbs.

What stands out in my mind to this day was how quickly she went from leading an intense workshop environment, with words of love and plenty of falling tears, to straddling and wrangling a mighty pine into submission with deafening machines.

She reinvented herself to be who she needed to be without missing a beat. In that moment, I realized this is what I was practicing to master myself. To be so present that whosoever I needed to be, I could quickly and effortlessly be that person. This, to me, was powerfully living in the moment.

ON THE RUNAWAY
TRAIN OF WANTING[*]

Before going off to train in a Zen monastery, my life could be summed up by this process:

- Become excited by something.
- Pursue that something.
- Get that something.
- Become obsessed with getting more of that something.

Then I would keep looping around-and-around doing that process all the time.

Here is an illustration of how this played out.

I was an artist who loved to create. I had a great job that paid extremely well. I only had to work part-time to be able to afford the beautiful apartment I lived in, pay the bills, purchase the food, and buy the stuff I collected continually. I told people I was working part-time so I could spend my free time on my artwork, "my passion in life."

Here's the funny, or rather the frustrating, part. Whenever I managed some free time – time I had explicitly created so I could focus on my artwork – I felt compelled to avoid doing it. Sometimes I would get as far as putting up a blank sheet of paper on the drawing board and proceed to stare at it. Then I would leave the apartment to shop for records. Or books. Or art supplies. Or all of them. I would spend most of the day shopping.

Then I'd come home, put on one of the new CDs I bought, begin listening to it and then...it would happen...

My head would explode, "Wow! This music is amazing! I need more of this! What else is out there like this?" And then I'd be off to the races again. I'd be looking up that information, calling around to see who had it. The music was playing in the background, and I didn't care. I was out on the streets hunting down more of it.

This insanity was non-stop.

I even started to do this process with the meditation books I discovered. I began collecting all of them, which is how I realized it was happening. The meditation books were teaching me about the process of dissatisfaction, and here I was live in 3-D, Technicolor and Surround Sound perpetuating that very process while becoming aware of it!

After meditating and having this insight, I sat there dumbstruck. I saw the addiction. "Oh my God! I have been doing my whole life like this!"

Everything flashed before my eyes. I saw all the times I was eating my meal and thinking of the dessert I was going to eat afterward. I witnessed myself unable to read the book in my hands because I was obsessed with thoughts of the movie I was going to watch with my friends the following day. I saw myself talking to a good friend and knew all I was thinking about was shopping for more music.

I was on the runaway train of "wanting" in the pursuit of "having." It was never going to give me what I longed for because I was never present to what I had. I was on to the next thing, never in the moment, and so joy was always evading me. I began to cry when I realized what was going on. I was on the wrong train going in the wrong direction.

Once I began meditating, I was able to articulate how I felt. I described my life as being stuck in an invisible box with myself while life was happening "out there" around me. I was always out of touch with it. It was always beyond my reach. Nothing was meaningful, conversations were shallow, I was hiding behind my mask of interests, and I wasn't enjoying anything I thought I should. What's worse, I saw that everyone else was caught up in doing the same thing, or his or her version of it. I realized that we are all completely screwed up and pretending like everything was just fine.

When I saw how it all worked, I realized I didn't want to play this game anymore.

That's why I say people can try to convince you to pursue your passions, to get what you want. They can tell you that when you do something satisfying, it will lead to an extraordinary life.

But I learned that this isn't the way it worked.

I realized I needed to learn firsthand how to be satisfied so I could lead an extraordinary life.

I needed to start, end, and be with satisfaction if I was to experience satisfaction. It wasn't the other way around.

MY INSIGHT STORY[†]

The setting for one of my greatest insights is at the monastery where I trained. It was early morning, and I was walking along the path from my hermitage to the main building. As I passed the clothesline area, I noticed a piece of trash by the side of the path.

Instantly, I had the impulse to pick up the trash. But on the heels of that impulse, I heard in my head, "Nah, don't bother. You didn't leave that there. Let the inattentive monk who dropped it there come back for it and deal with it. Why are you always picking up after others? Besides, you've got to get to the building. You're the breakfast cook. Don't waste your time with this..."

So, what did I do? The only "rational thing" I could: I listened to the voices, believed them, and just kept walking.

As I rounded the fence to get to the building, my teacher passed me on the path. She immediately noticed the trash, called my attention to it and asked me if I'd seen it there.

This was a real rock-and-a-hard-place moment for me.

If I said no, I was basically confessing to being an inattentive, unconscious, bad Zen monk who was lost in his thoughts so much that he was oblivious to his surroundings – including that piece of trash!

If I said yes, then the next logical question from my teacher would be, "Well, why on earth would you not pick it up? Why would you ignore it and keep walking?" In essence, why didn't I take responsibility for it?

Since I took a vow not to tell lies nor practice believing the fantasies of authority – and truthfully because I had been nailed – I told her what happened:

"I was bamboozled by the voices in my head."

To recap how all of this works:

An insight dropped in to pick up the trash. Insights are quick, complete, and perfect. No manipulation, debating, or lengthy dissertations. Insights are the still small voices that remind you to grab your keys if you're on your way to drive your car. They come up with brilliant ideas for your next book while you're in the shower. If you allow them to, insights can generally guide your life perfectly.

Insights show up in a flash and are often short and illuminating.

On the other hand, the voices elbow themselves in and, in my story, they cajoled me out of doing what I knew was right. All sorts of excuses and "good reasons" surfaced. The quality and the structure of conditioned mind is exactly the opposite of insight. In fact, conditioned mind and the voices attempt to override insight at every turn by obscuring the insight and redirecting my attention to discursive thought.

The end result: I felt bad for knowing better and not doing better.

Can you see this in your own life? This is what the voices do when we make commitments and have insights. The voices:

- Trick us out of keeping commitments or following through on insights;
- Sweep in to beat us up when something goes wrong as a result of believing them;
- High-five each other and proclaim, "Mission accomplished!" Not only did they bamboozle us out of doing what we knew to do, but they blamed us for the whole thing.

Luckily the monastery was a safe place where I had the opportunity to explore how this all worked. This is exactly what our training entailed. My teacher and all the other monks were on my team conspiring to help me get it. It was up to me to see how insights appeared and to see how the voices worked to sabotage me from following those insights.

The ultimate goal is to catch the voices in action and choose something else. The ideal is to expose them earlier until we can no longer be fooled. Then to live from insights and compassionate self-mentoring full-time.

WHAT ARE THE VOICES?

Ever since we were little, we've been conditioned to fit into society. We had to become something else for the big people to accept us. We had to leave who we were naturally. To an extent, that's good. It's what keeps us from tossing our food at each other in restaurants. But the process of socialization we experienced was brutal.

To keep us in line, we got punished and rewarded. How we were treated was quite conditional. By the time socialization was complete, "the voices" in our heads were put in charge of punishing and rewarding us to replace the big people. These voices are obviously still in charge of us today. They are watching us to keep us in line and they'll beat us up as necessary. "For our sake. To protect us."

What's missing, and what all of us are craving desperately, is acceptance. An experience of you accepted exactly as you are. One-hundred percent. With unconditional love.

THE WONDERFUL
WORLD OF EMOTIONS

Sorrow prepares you for joy. It violently sweeps everything out of your house, so that new joy can find space to enter. It shakes the yellow leaves from the bough of your heart, so that fresh, green leaves can grow in their place. It pulls up the rotten roots, so that new roots hidden beneath have room to grow. Whatever sorrow shakes from your heart, far better things will take their place.
—Rumi

Emotions are like the currents that run through the power cables of your energy system. Movement is desirable and emotions are nothing but pure movement.

When the mind becomes involved, it has the incredible ability to interfere with the natural flow of this movement. It will set up an emotion to loop over-and-over again by triggering a story to repeat.

I remember in grade school I had a habit of developing a boyish crush on some girl and then I would lament about how she did not love me. I'd go to the swing set in my backyard alone and cry for what seemed like hours. As soon as the story of how she did not love me lost steam, I replayed the story so I could begin crying again. That's when I learned it was possible for me to keep myself disabled in an emotion for an indefinite period of time. Because if I ever "forgot" to feel this emotion I was addicted to (sadness) and found myself running around happy again (heaven forbid!), I would simply replay that story. Cause and effect.

At the Zen monastery we had a young woman who came to train for a short while. Whenever she would sit down to meditate, she would soon begin to cry. And it would go on for most of the meditation. It continued to happen at every meditation. I remember the head monk sought guidance from our teacher on this situation. On the one hand, she could have been releasing emotions bottled up for years and this was her opportunity to complete the process. On the other hand, and this is what was revealed through her guidance appointment, she kept repeating the story that created the emotions. Eventually she was asked to leave. She decided to choose suffering by indulging it. She chose to hold on instead of let go.

Infants and young children have shown me that emotions are extremely transient. It's startling how quick a pure emotion will move through their system and then be released for the next one. This is why you'll see a toddler stumble, fall, scream bloody murder (there wasn't even any blood!) and then in the next moment jump up, run and laugh again. Ready for action. Like nothing ever happened.

To me, this is our natural state. To have the ability to reinvent our emotions, thoughts, and perceptions of life from moment-to-moment. Sorrow, laughter, frustration, passion, boredom all pass and give wake to the next most interesting life experience available and waiting for us – if we allow them to.

A SHIFT TO LOVE

"**B**ut what about your savings for when you retire? Aren't you concerned about your future?"

My father and I were standing in the kitchen arguing about my decision to train in a Zen monastery. I'd been there for over two years and every time we'd see each other, we would inadvertently go "here" in the conversation. His main objection was that I wasn't out in the world making money, putting it away toward what I might need. No 401(k). From his point of view, this was prime time for me to be working and saving money, while I was in my 30s.

I would yell back at him, "But there is no future! There is only *now*!" which would cause him to look at me like I was the biggest fool in the world.

I hated this stupid argument. He was just trying to drive me crazy and control me, like he and my mother had been trying to do for years. This was a senseless battle. He would never understand my point of view and I would certainly never adopt his fear-based one.

I looked over at him standing beside the sink, shaking his head in disbelief, and then it fell in. The insight dropped in and I spoke it out loud. I knew I was talking out loud because he turned to look at me suddenly.

I blurted, "Omigod! You're saying all of this because you *love* me. Not because you hate me or you're trying to drive me crazy or control me. You *love* me!"

He looked at me and I looked at him for what seemed like an eternity. I can't tell which one of us broke down first, because the only thing I remember next is that I was hugging him and tears streamed out of our eyes. He said, "Of course I love you. Both Mom and I love you very much. We just want the best for you." And I was repeating, "Thank you. I love you. I know. Thank you." We stood crying in each other's arms.

You have to understand that this had never happened before. My dad and I never expressed anything remotely emotional with each other. Ever. Now, here we were, open and vulnerable. Telling each other that we loved one another.

All because of a shift.

A shift in perspective. A way of seeing that wasn't available a moment before. One that allowed me to see the truth and to speak it out loud. To change a relationship between my father and me forever.

You see, it wasn't a tactic or a plot to bring us together. I didn't learn how to create great relationships at the Zen monastery where I was training. And I'm not sharing this with you now so you can go to the person you're fighting with and try this "technique" out on them. That's what I see in everything I read about in personal development. They all tell you to "Do this. Do that. Say this. Say that. Manipulate this. Manipulate that." All surface level "changes" that rearrange with no depth or understanding.

What no one realizes (and what I didn't realize) is we need to *un*learn all this information we've been taught so we can be present with what is. With who is. With ourselves. With Life.

So we can *see. Hear. Feel. Touch. Taste. Smell. Love. Be With.* All of it.

The reason people see me and experience me as a grounded person who responds and is present with them is that *I'm here.* Presence is not something you can learn. It's something you must *shift* into. Like the "ah-ha" of a puzzle piece clicking into place when you stop trying so hard.

You don't have to change a thing in your life to experience everything as completely different. When I was in that kitchen with my father, we were still the same people we were a moment before. Two people with the same opinions and values. I went back to train at the monastery for another decade and he wished that I was out in the world making money.

What changed was this: I suddenly saw what was missing between us and what I could never unsee.

Love.

TWO WAYS

Imagine a group of football players huddled in front a video of themselves playing a game. Notice their coach in the room with them. They're studying the plays and learning from what they observe. "Oh, look at that! We needed to focus on defense here!" or "She needed to take two more steps there before throwing the ball…" This is a very high-energy, enthusiastic application of what happened to determine how they can go *forward*.

Now, this is very helpful. This is very loving and compassionate because they are using the information to get better.

What would not be helpful is for certain team players to be judged and berated because of what happened, or made to feel bad, shamed or criticized due to what they were watching. "Coulda, woulda, shoulda." That won't help them or the team improve. That would shut everyone down and make them self-conscious. This is a very low-energy, degrading application of what happened. It dwells in the *past* and creates barriers to anything better being done in the future.

Consider these two relationships.

Choose the one you want to have with yourself and others.

Practice that one.

A NEW WAY

 I cannot destroy evil out there. Evil doesn't exist out there.

Evil is an idea that exists in my own heart.

It's the anger I have toward those who hate. Toward those who harm my family or those who harm innocent beings, the planet, or justice, or whatever I care about.

Evil is anything that threatens my identity, threatens my existence or gets between me and what I want. I feel it inside of me and I become angry. I want to destroy it because it feels more potent than this fear I experience.

Anger is a powerful motivator. It is what drove me to the Zen monastery where I trained in the first place.

I didn't go there because "I was so in love with my life." But love is what kept me there all those years, and it gave me a voice to express a new way of being.

Love became my creative force.

I learned that I could hate suffering, or I could love freedom. I could beat myself into overcoming resistance, or I could love myself into living my dreams. You may call it a matter of semantics, but for me, I say that how you do what you do is everything.

It either poisons or nourishes.

Separates or unifies.

Holds together or dissolves.

Evil into love.

NO YOU DO NOT
BEAT YOURSELF UP

One of the most unfortunate lies people believe is that they beat themselves up.

I hear it all the time. It will inadvertently come out of people's mouths while I'm talking to them.

"I want to work on my project, but I don't, and then I beat myself up for that..."

I interject, "No you don't. You absolutely *do not* beat yourself up. That's not what's going on."

The person will typically pause, and then I'll continue to explain, "Look, you're being beaten up. You don't wake up in the morning and say to yourself, 'I wonder how many people I can make upset with me today. I wonder what I can royally screw up today. I wonder how awful of a person I can be today, so that I can later beat myself up.' No. You actually want to do the best you can, given how you see the world.

"What happens is this: You 'make a mistake,' and then the voices pounce on you. They say, 'Look at you! What a loser! No one likes you! You'll never get this right! You say you want to work on your project, but you spend your time on Facebook...' and then the voices 'Beat You Up.' Can you picture it?"

For a moment, I can tell they can see the logic behind the scenario I'm describing. Yet even after they understand what the voices are and how they work, I'll still catch the phrase coming out of their mouths. "I beat myself up."

It's an incredibly pervasive notion that we do something as ridiculous as "beat ourselves up," like we're the unnamed narrator from the movie *Fight Club*, who literally punches himself in the face.

Let's put this phrase to rest from our language so we can describe it the way it really happens. So we can stop taking the blame for the abuse and start taking action by overturning the abusers who hide in our subconscious.

I'm convinced that this simple shift will transform your relationship with yourself forever.

AUTHOR YOUR THOUGHTS

 If you examine your thoughts, you will begin to notice a fascinating thing:

Most of them are not your own.

You don't consciously author them.

Many will drop in, boss you around, convince you of things, rob you of your attention, make you feel bad and essentially waste your time.

To "author your thoughts" requires that you sincerely pay attention. Only by being here in this moment do you have the opportunity to author your thoughts and direct your attention.

To create instead of follow.

To respond instead of react.

To awaken instead of suffer.

WHERE YOUR ATTENTION GOES, SO GOES YOUR LIFE

What you keep your attention on flourishes. And keeping your attention focused on what you want takes conscious effort.

Have you ever noticed how easy it is to allow a garden to become overgrown with weeds? It does so without any effort on your part. The vegetables, fruits, and flowers start to do poorly when you don't water them, stop giving them nutrients, or allow bugs and gophers to chomp on them.

Indulging habits and unconsciousness is a lot like allowing a garden to fall apart.

However, when you focus on what supports the garden, what takes care of the plants and what allows them to flourish, you bring mindful, conscious, compassionate attention to your life.

It's not that doing these things makes you a "good person" and not doing them makes you a "bad person." It's that you get different results by doing them versus not doing them.

Where is your attention? Where would you like it to be?

What do you want to flourish?

Now put your attention there.

Kindness is not coming home after a hard day of work and turning on the TV, plopping down on the couch and downing a tub of ice cream when you committed to meditating.

The voices will say, "Oh you deserve it! Take a break! Stop being so hard on yourself..."

If you buy into their game and go along with their bad advice, you'll later be beaten up for listening to them – especially when your meditation practice is gone, and you're struggling again.

That doesn't mean you can't come home, turn on the TV, plop down on the couch and have some ice cream.

You just choose to do it consciously. Mindfully, compassionately and with full awareness.

In this way, you create integrity in your life. You stop being led around by the nose by those unhelpful voices.

When you consciously create and keep your commitments, you are proclaiming you are in charge of your life and you are a trustworthy steward of it.

That's the ultimate kindness.

IF IT'S WORTH DOING

What I loved about the training I received at the Zen monastery was the encouragement to be deliberate in every thought and every deed.

So instead of haphazardly sticking a stamp onto an envelope, we were shown to neatly and precisely place it into the corner of the envelope. When doing messy work, we carefully laid drop cloths and were mindful of our surroundings. Everything deserved our loving attention and consideration.

When speaking to other monks or facilitating groups, we brought intention to our every word. Nothing was out of place.

We were encouraged to give what was right in front of us our full, undivided attention. If it was worth doing, it was worth using both hands.

We were shown to revere all of life, and in so doing, we revered ourselves. The outer was not different than the inner.

Love for the stamp is love for the self.

THE JOY OF CARING

We become compassionate not from altruism, which denies the self for the sake of the other, but from the insight that sees and feels one IS the other.
—Huston Smith

It was early morning, and the night before there was a huge rainstorm. A light mist was still falling when I approached the monastery's main building. From just behind the hill I could make out that there were several other monks, still in their raincoats, walking back and forth along the porch. I could see they were doing something unusual. They were kneeling down to pick something up off the porch and put it into a bucket. As I got closer, I could see they were collecting the earthworms that crawled up onto the tiles from the courtyard.

I wiped my shoes on the mat and proceeded to the coat rack to unload my backpack. One of the monks in a yellow coat approached me, bowed to me, and showed me a note. I returned the bow and realized it was the Guestmaster. The soggy note said, "We are collecting worms from the porch and putting them into the bucket. Please assist. In Lovingkindness, Guestmaster." I bowed to acknowledge that I had read the note and moved in with the rest of the monks. I picked up the remaining stray worms off the porch and put them into the bucket of soil. As I saw how frail the worms were and how kind the monks were to them, I began to cry. Where on the planet could I have ever gone to see people who were stopping to help a creature that seemed so insignificant?

I continued to see and participate in similar acts of kindness during my training. A baby bat that had fallen from the eaves was assisted back up to its mother. Tadpoles trapped in a puddle while we were building the pond in our courtyard were relocated to a bucket of water. Wild animals that were injured or sick were driven to the local vet for care.

While I was at the monastery, I learned the joy of caring. I experienced that caring was not a duty, obligation, or tedious chore to be done but rather an opportunity to open my heart and serve at a deeper level.

Caring for the earthworms for the sake of the earthworms. Caring for the bats for the sake of the bats. Caring for the carrots for the sake of the carrots.

In caring for them, I cared for myself. No deed there was, no doer thereof. I was not separate from all of life. Everything was a mirror for my relationship with myself. I saw how putting a stamp neatly into the corner of an envelope deliberately was a metaphor for how I treated myself.

Nothing was insignificant.

WHAT'S IN THIS FOR ME?*

At the Zen monastery we made a distinction between "bringing spiritual practice into our lives" versus "bringing our lives into spiritual practice."

You see, if I am using spiritual practice (mindfulness, meditation, chanting, visualizations, breathing techniques, etc.) to better my life, subtly I'm saying I must improve myself. I need to get something for myself that I'm somehow lacking. It's like the ego is proclaiming, "What's in this for *me*?"

In our modern-day world, we can be incredibly results driven. So it's easy to see why we would approach even spiritual practices in this manner. I mean, why do something if we don't get the good stuff from it? Where's the R.O.I.? Right?

However, in my experience, there's a different attitude of mind we can take. We can bring our lives *into* spiritual practice.

For me, this approach represents humility, surrender, and trust. It's like I'm saying, "Life, you know best. I don't have any control over this transformation business. I am going to get out of the way so you can live through me perfectly." In this way, my most significant contribution to Life is to show up fully, do my work, and leave the results to the Universe.

Take, for example, the humble caterpillar. It doesn't go out and say, "I'm going to make this transformation business happen for me by becoming a better being. I'm going to become a butterfly, gosh, darn it!" On the contrary, that caterpillar has Life on its side to deal with the *how* of transformation. The only thing the caterpillar needs to do is keep showing up and keep doing what it does to facilitate the process. For the caterpillar, the transformation is *inevitable.*

Look to see how you can be like that caterpillar. Surrender to your practice. Bring your life *into* your spiritual practice.

Allow Life to surprise you.

BLESSINGS IN DISGUISE

Everything that's happened in the past has prepared me to be who I am now. Just as what's happening now is preparing me for who I am to become. I never know the end of the story.

Before finding the practice and becoming a Zen teacher, my teacher was extremely depressed – so depressed that she put a shotgun to her midsection and pulled the trigger when she was 18. The surgeon who sewed her up and saved her life told her she should not have survived the blast. He encouraged her to discover why she was still alive. His advice made a deep impression on her.

After her recovery, she embarked on a search for the meaning of life, or at least the meaning of her own life. She started by exploring religions and ultimately fell in love with Zen. As chance would have it, there was a Zen monastery close to where she was living, which in those days was nothing short of a miracle. She went to train there for many years and later founded a Zen monastery of her own.

Many years later, she and her community are now helping

people all over the world transform lives and end suffering. Seekers travel from across the globe to participate in meditation and awareness retreats. Technology closes the gap between those who want relief and the teachings. Even children in an African village are eating meals daily because of her.

In public talks, my teacher shocks audiences with her story about the depression that drove her to suicide. She would call depression her greatest ally, a worthy opponent that helped motivate her to stay conscious and aware. If she indulged the voices in her head for even a moment, she would become lost in depression's grip – something she wasn't willing to allow.

But here's what stood out for me in her talks: She never wished that anyone had stopped her from pulling the trigger. In a world that fears death, making mistakes, experiencing "bad" emotions and choosing the wrong path, her message was compelling to me.

When I considered the magnitude of what she was saying, I saw that her attempted suicide resulted in so much incredible goodness that may never have come about had she not done the unthinkable.

Her message was a reminder for me never to forget: We don't know how the story will end. There are no such things as "mistakes." We mustn't become paralyzed by meanings drawn from circumstances.

I can look back at my own life and see horrible situations that resulted in powerful turning points. And this, in turn, helps me to consider current struggles as possible preparations for something better.

Tragedy can be a blessing in disguise.

Like bliss arising from sorrow.

Like a lotus blossoming from the muck.

EVOKING WHO YOU ARE BEING[†]

There are two parts inside of you with whom you can be in a conversation.

The part that experiences limitation, fear, small-ness, anger, wrong, depression, and separation, and the part that experiences possibility, excitement, vastness, joy, confidence, and power. In fact, these two parts live in the only two places we can place our attention at any given moment. In my training, we referred to these places as "The Dark Room" and "The Light Room."

I find that my life devolves when I stay in dark room conversations. These conversations aren't going anywhere. They're the downward spirals of the ego.

As a matter of fact, if I stay within the superficial aspects of my client's life and get tangled up in the details – the dramas and the dysfunction – my attention to them will ruin the coaching session. That's because the ego has no real interest in anything shifting. Oftentimes it just wants to be right, left alone, or in the company of other gripers, whiners, and misery-makers who reside in The Dark Room.

However, through the power of directing a person's attention, I can speak to the aspects of this person who live in The Light Room. Sometimes this shift appears to be like a magic trick. I start speaking and the person begins to feel better, more motivated, see new horizons and transform. That's because I have been actively engaging and directing my conversation to the part of them with whom I want to speak: The person who operates in The Light Room. In a sense, I am disidentifying them from the ego, the smaller parts of themselves, and the self-hatred. I'm evoking their authentic being instead.

I am having a direct conversation with the power that animates them.

I'll never forget a coaching session I did with a client who started our conversation criticizing the actions of her partner around the holidays. She was not seeing all the assumptions she was making about his possible motivations. She was dead set upon proving to me how he was wrong and she was right. Now, if I decided to get involved in this, to show her what I was seeing, I would either end up as "the enemy" (taking his side), "the advisor" (giving my unwanted opinion) or "the idiot" (not understanding her point of view). Instead, I asked her some questions directed to the part of her who wasn't identified with the blame. For instance, I asked her, "Why do you think he did that?" This simple question encouraged her to stand in his shoes and begin to see another perspective. I asked, "What else?" so we could get even more perspectives.

As she answered my questions, she began to see for herself the story she had created based on her assumptions. Then I asked her, "Do you think he loves you?" at which point she said, "Yes, of course," and then the tears came, as well as some clarity around how she felt for him and her disappointment. We got to the heart of the issue without dealing with the smoke-and-mirrors "problem."

This wasn't just a "relationship with her partner" issue. This was a beingness issue. A relationship with herself issue.

We then focused on her and the creative part of her who could solve this "problem." The part of her who was empowered and saw possibilities. The part that operated from creativity, love, and joy.

This was the part who could create solutions.

The part who desperately needs to be in charge of being her full time.

In our work together, I helped her access this part of herself over and over again until she felt like she could be that part more and more often. When she learned to master choosing who she was being, which room she was occupying – The Dark Room or The Light Room – everything else in her life began to open up in exactly the same manner.

She put the part of her who needed to be in charge of her life in charge.

That made all the difference.

Have you noticed this trend?

When things get challenging or when you experience a setback, the immediate impulse is to drop all the support you have in your life and descend into negativity.

A breakup, a tough day at work, a promotion that didn't go through, a flat tire, another mass shooting, something political that hurts your heart...

Then suddenly everything you care about and all your support structures get dropped. And with them, your energy siphons off too.

Hopelessness and depression fall over you. As a result, you lose everything. You stop taking care of yourself. You get buried under the voices. You stop exercising, stop eating well, stop meditating, stop getting enough sleep, start eating sugar and start drinking a bunch of coffee.

You drop all the things that support your heart.

Suddenly you're depleted.

It's much harder to choose love when you're in this depleted condition.

However, love can accomplish a great deal. It's why there's so much resistance to it from the voices.

If you care about principles and causes like protecting the environment, human rights or animal rights, then you want to take every bit of life force you've got and infuse them with love.

Bring your love to what is important to you.

The Buddha told his disciples:

Just as a mother with her own life protects her only child from harm, so let your love flow outward to the universe. A limitless love without hatred or enmity.

If you have children you love, you know you don't want to let your depression debilitate you. You need lots of love to care for them. This is *exactly* the time to be strong and say *"No"* to the voices. This is *exactly* the time you need to care for yourself like that child because you're counting on you. We're counting on you.

It's the same with loving the world. You can't love the world by being defeated or hopeless. Your suffering will not help a single suffering person.

You don't want to waste a second of it trying to figure out who you should exclude or who is worthy of it. You simply love.

HOW TO STAY GROUNDED

The secret to staying grounded is simple:

Don't indulge the thinking. Don't noodle the juicy story.

Don't leave the ground.

Nothing is more important than presence. Your heart does not resist your body coming to silence. Only the voices of resistance want you to leave the peace that is who you authentically are to visit the mind's Crazy Fun House of distorted mirrors and shifting floors.

Why?

So you can frantically search for peace – the peace you had before you left. The peace that is you.

Stay at Center and allow everything to come to you. Never leave Center to indulge a problem, a concern, or a worry.

Center is where your power is.

ALEX MILL

Chasing after the world brings chaos.
Allowing it all to come to me brings peace.
—Zen Gatha

CHEERING YOU ON TO SUCCESS

Are you being cheered on? Or put down in life?

Since we've been little, we've had this really awful voice inside our heads that is in charge of judging and punishing us so that we do good and be better people. Unfortunately, keeping this voice intact within us has had really negative consequences.

What I've found is that no one actually performs better when they're being judged, punished, or made miserable. In my experience it makes them timid, rigid, and fearful. People don't learn or take the risks necessary to get better. They play safe to avoid "mistakes" rather than taking risks that expand them. They avoid failing, feeling bad, being hurt, or let down. To (hopefully) avoid those wake-them-up-in-the-middle-of-the-night reviews from the voices. The ones that outline "where they ought to be and how they're not measuring up."

The problem is there's nothing to counter this barrage, nothing inside of us that is encouraging, drawing us forward, supporting us, or cheering us on.

Have you noticed?

Take a marathon for example. At a marathon or a race, you'll see crowds of people cheering the runners along, rooting them on and giving them water at certain breakpoints. They'll yell, "You can do it! Keep going!" There is no one making anyone feel bad at a race. Because that would be demoralizing and an energy suck. That heckler would get thrown out!

But where is that support within you when you need it?

What you have instead is a crappy voice that will evaluate you and make you feel bad.

There is an enormous distinction between the voices in our heads and our Inner Mentor. This distinction is the basis of what I teach. It's at the heart of the coaching I do and the programs I offer. It's what I learned during my training.

I'm passionate about helping people dismantle the voices that keep them limited. It excites me to see them put a part of themselves in charge of their lives who is wiser, stronger, kinder and more supportive. Someone I call the compassionate Inner Mentor.

It's the grown-up you've always wanted to be there with you all throughout life, guiding you with conscious, compassionate awareness. Cheering you on and helping you succeed.

EVERY LIABILITY
HAS ITS SUPERPOWER

I've had strings of conversations with clients who confessed to me that they struggle with "perfectionism." They tell me this as though it's something shameful. And I say, "So what's the problem with that?" To this, they typically reply, "Well, it really keeps me stuck."

First of all, let's be clear that no way of being is a problem. It's only a problem when the voices in your head get a hold of it and make it a source of suffering.

When the voices get a hold of perfectionism, they focus not on what's "perfect," but rather on what's imperfect. They prevent you from taking action because whatever you're doing will never measure up to their elusive standards. It will never be good enough. This conversation creates the feeling of being stuck. The fear of not measuring up induces procrastination and paralysis.

However, when your *heart* gets a hold of perfectionism, that's something else. I bet your heart has made some pure magic for you. I've asked my "perfectionist" clients, "Can you recall a time when perfectionism served you?" I'll never forget one client who belted out a long list of achievements, "It helped me train for my marathon, it got me into law school, it helped me excel at tests, it launched my new business, it bought the perfect gift for my best friend's wedding shower..."

She *got* it! Lots of love to the Perfectionist, right?!

Even judgment and comparison can be converted into gold. Judgment and comparison from the voices create misery and suffering, but judgment and comparison from the *heart* create discernment and inspiration.

The process is *everything*.

Instantly, it creates realignment. Alchemy is in the shift.

So how can you tap into accessing your superpowers all the time? How can you convert lead into gold?

What you need at the outset is someone in charge of operating from Center. The part of you who is The Director, The Conductor, The Adult, The Leader, The Wise Person on the Mountain, Yoda, Your compassionate Inner Mentor. Whatever you want to call this person, he or she is the part of you that you want in charge of your whole life.

This part scans the horizon and whom to give the appropriate job. So when it's time to relax, you get the "Happy-Go-Lucky" part of you to go enjoy yourself, without the voices that yell, "Look at you! You're so lazy. Not getting anything productive done. You're letting your coach down." Likewise, when it's time to be productive and work, you get the "Focused Creator" part of you to go make stuff happen, not the voices that yell, "Look at you! You're neglecting your family. You should be out enjoying the beautiful day. All work and no play makes Johnny a dull boy."

From Center, you can create a beautiful life.

How will you shift? What's a weakness for you? Where and when has that weakness been a strength?

When you find something, don't stop examining. You'll surprise yourself if you keep digging.

Bryan Franklin, a top entrepreneur and executive coach, once determined that his weakness was "laziness." Because of his laziness, he developed a knack for finding shortcuts. Eventually, he transformed his "weakness" into a superpower by creating software automation systems (shortcuts!) to reduce the amount of work people had to do. And his automation systems made him very successful.

So don't stop looking. Your superpower awaits you in the last place you'd look.

THREE ELEMENTS
OF A SPIRITUAL PRACTICE

H ere are what I consider to be the three elements of a
spiritual practice:

1. Where your attention goes, so goes your life, just like the
    Buddha taught. So, if you want to have peace, joy, and hap-
    piness you must keep your attention on peace, joy, and hap-
    piness. Because one process does not lead to another. I
    learned this in my personal practice when I discovered that
    wanting does not lead to having. Wanting simply leads to
    more wanting (more dissatisfaction). Only having fulfill-
    ment will lead to having an experience of fulfillment.

2. Once you learn how to train your attention through Zen
    meditation, the next step is to keep it on what supports
    you. Instead of allowing your attention to habitually wander
    off with the negative voices swirling around in your head,
    you must keep your attention on the loving, compassionate,

and wise mentor inside of you who can guide you through life perfectly.

3. Lastly, it takes another person who is further along on the path than you and a group of people who are practicing around you to keep the practice alive within you. It's too difficult to do this work in isolation. This is why Buddhism teaches that Sangha (community) is one of the three jewels of spiritual practice, along with the Buddha (the example) and the Dharma (the teachings). It's why I love to participate in communities where people are supporting each other and we're all attempting to do the same thing.

HUNTING PANIC ATTACKS

"If it weren't for you, I'd probably be curled up on Prozac somewhere right now."

I was astonished to hear Andrea, my former client, say this to me.

We were on the phone talking about what her life was like currently. I made some flippant remark about what we were working on together at the time, and this was her retort.

I hadn't spoken to Andrea for over three years. She and I had helped her achieve what she wanted through our coaching a few years before. I had seen some photos she'd been posting on Facebook. She looked fabulous. She was thriving. Her life seemed incredible and I wanted to experience what it would be like to talk to her now. I had reached out and suggested this phone conversation so we could catch up.

I met Andrea at one of my meditation workshops, back when I first came out of the monastery. She sent me an email to see if it would be possible to work with me one-on-one. On our first phone call she sounded like she was full of anxiety. She told me she had panic attacks at least once every week. That's why she was interested in meditation – to see if meditation could help her. To see if she could do something about her panic attacks that didn't involve drugs. She had been stressed before, but when the panic attacks started, they threw her over the edge. They came on unexpectedly. She was terrified of them taking over her entire life.

I slowed Andrea down and explained to her that I wasn't a therapist. I told her how coaching was different. But after hearing her distress, I reassured her that I could help her. My Zen training showed me how the mind worked and what was happening to her was no different than any other problem. We could get her panic attacks sorted out and then work to make her life better in a lot of different ways from there. I asked her if that sounded good.

She was relieved and sighed, "Yes."

I began to tell her about the voices in her head, something I mentioned at the workshop. I asked her to explain to me what the voices were saying to her about her panic attacks. What did she hear in her head the moment they began? What did they say while the panic attacks were going on? How did that feel?

I kept exploring Andrea's thoughts and asked her questions until we mapped out the entire process.

Once we laid it out for her to see, her homework assignment was simple.

"Go hunting voices."

"What?" she asked.

I said, "You're going to go hunting voices. Instead of them pursuing you and hunting you – jumping you when you least expect them, bringing on the panic attacks – you're going to go after them. We're going to turn the tables on them!" I was excited and couldn't hide my enthusiasm.

There was a pause on the other end of the phone.

I continued, "Set the alarm on your phone to go off every 20 minutes. Every time it goes off, I want you to look to see where the panic attack is. Do you think you can do that?"

After another pause, she said, "Yes, I can do this." Then I asked, "*Will* you do this?" And she said instantly, "Yes, I will do this. If this will stop the panic attacks, I'll do anything."

I said, "Excellent! I want you to stay in touch with me to let me know how it's going. Will you do that too? Can you send me a report in a couple of days?" She agreed.

When I got her emails, it was clear that Andrea was on top of those voices. I was impressed. She was apparently a woman of action and her determination freed her from a complete mental and emotional collapse. She was going after those voices like her life depended on it.

Because she was paying such close attention, there was no possible way a panic attack could happen. Panic attacks take over when we are unaware. She became hyper-aware in a big hurry.

That "panic attack project" was just the first of many beautiful things we did together. The rest of our work over the coming months was spent focusing on her business, getting her out of school (collecting degrees) and into creating a lifestyle she would love. She was also doing my 30-day online retreat on self-compassion in between our weekly sessions. This helped to fortify herself from the inside out when I wasn't around.

Andrea truly blossomed.

When we hung up the phone, I was so happy for her. She gave me lots of credit for helping her get to where she is, but I can honestly say that it was because of her incredible willingness to take a stand for herself that the transformation happened.

Here is a perfect illustration of the three principles of a spiritual practice: Andrea learned to direct her attention through meditation and by hunting the voices. She kept her attention on what would support her by learning compassionate self-mentoring. And she got the assistance she needed from someone who could assist her through the process. Each element worked together to guide her to create the life she wanted for herself.

WHO HAS THE LAST WORD?[†]

For every action you take, there's some kind of feedback you get.

Cook beans. Turn out well.
Feedback: "Good cook."

Cook beans. Burn.
Feedback: "Bad cook."

What matters most is who has the last word.

Whose ultimate feedback will you listen to? On which side of the fence will you land? On the side that brings you down, makes you feel bad, calls you an idiot and ruins your day? Or the side that encourages you to try again, keep going, learn more and move on to the next adventure?

Understanding who has the last word is a powerful distinction to cultivate.

One side hates you.
The other side loves you.
How about you?
Who has the last word?

THE PRACTICE OF NO REVIEWS

We had a guideline at the monastery that specifically helped senior monks who facilitated group discussions. It was called, "No Reviews."

The way it worked was after every group we facilitated, we were encouraged not to entertain the voices in our heads, which had us replay how our facilitation went. Such ruminations typically led to "train wrecks." We'd wish we had said something more clever. Or that we had performed better. Or we'd think we just ruined someone's life because of what we said.

Anytime we would catch ourselves engaging in this kind of discursive thought (which was very tempting to do), we would drop it like a sack of hot potatoes and practice presence instead.

The principle maintained that if there were any insights we were to have about our facilitation, we would have received them *in the moment*. We would *know* what was skillful and what wasn't. We would know in a flash how to improve our facilitation.

Plus, all of our group discussions were recorded and we were asked to listen to the recording later on, at a time when we could sit together with our loving, wise, compassionate Inner Mentor. To listen with full awareness, consciousness, and attention.

As you move through your days, I encourage you to embrace the principle of "No Reviews" yourself. No feeling bad or regrets about the past. Nothing to rob you of this glorious present – where all the magic of creation exists. And if you are going to reflect upon what happened, be sure to have that wise, unconditionally loving Inner Mentor with you. This mentor sees how perfect you are *and* will help you become any way you want to be.

HOW TO
LIVE A MINDFUL, KINDFUL LIFE*

From my own personal observations, happiness does not seem to exist in the activities and things of this world. A person can dwell in paradise and be miserable while another person can live in squalor and be happy.

Happiness lives in our perspective of things and situations.

Happiness is a byproduct of where our attention goes.

I have also noticed there can be no internal shift to happiness without first changing how we behave. That is, we can't go on doing the same stuff that isn't working and expect different results.

This is why service was such an enormous component of my life when I was a monk. This is why St. Francis of Assisi put it perfectly when he said, *"Preach the Gospel at all times. Use words if necessary."*

Compassionate action is the necessary key to change my view of the world.

I had experience after experience of showing up wholeheartedly in life as the antidote to any challenge. While I was at the monastery,

I was the cook for many, many years. I could either show up and work day-in and day-out joyfully, or I could show up day-in and day-out miserably. The choice was entirely mine! I was showing up whether I was happy or not!

That's when it occurred to me to see my day as an imaginary pie divided up into slivers of moments. I knew I couldn't always choose what would fill those moments, but I could choose how I wanted to *be* in those moments. In the times when I *could* choose how to fill those moments, I would fill them with what supported me.

For example, today, when I wake up, I immediately sit and meditate. That's sliver one. Then I perform a simple ritual that involves yoga and a little chanting. That's sliver two. And then so on throughout my day.

Now doing the dishes shows up as one of those slivers too. I don't always want to do them, but I am going to do them anyway. This is when I ask myself, "How do I want to *be* while I'm doing the dishes?" Then I practice that.

And so on with the remaining slivers.

What slivers do you struggle with the most? How would you like to *be* that would change how you experience those slivers?

HOW TO
SIT STILL WITH EMOTIONS[*]

You are a buoy in the ocean.

Imagine the waters around you.

Sometimes they are gentle. Lapping against you.

At other times they are gigantic waves, crashing over you. Over and over. Unrelenting and violent.

Because they are the waters in the ocean.

But you stay put.

Because you are the buoy.

And that's just what the buoy and the waters do.

HOW TO
BREAK THOUGHT LOOPS

W hy are we conditioned to feel bad, experience resistance, focus on the negative, and sabotage ourselves?

The Buddha taught that thoughts create our reality and where we direct our attention determines the quality of our lives. We can either be here (present) or we can not be here (lost in thought and suffering).

As a monk, I practiced meditation and used the tools of awareness practice to expose the constructs of my mind. I discovered that the only limitations I experienced in life were created by my failure to understand how my mind worked. Because I didn't know how my mind worked, I kept falling into the same traps over and over again.

Back when cassette tapes were still around, it was easy to describe these mental patterns through the analogy of tape loops. Like one tape spliced to itself, it just kept repeating again and again.

Today, there is some scientific evidence that 95% of our thoughts today are the same ones we had yesterday, and that 80%

of those repeated thoughts are negative. Daniel Amen, an American celebrity doctor who practices as a psychiatrist and brain disorder specialist, calls them "automatic negative thoughts." ANTs for short. Many people I talk to can attest to this assertion, with or without the stats. So, what's the solution?

At the monastery we taught that these thought loops were operating in the background unconsciously and it was imperative for us to bring them to the surface into full consciousness. Once they were brought up to the surface, the next step was to have an effect on them. To interrupt them, stop them, and break them up – whatever was required, so when the tape played, it stopped sounding believable.

Only when we consciously interfered with it did we have a chance to successfully break free of it and create something new.

NO WAS NOT AN OPTION[*]

One of the biggest gifts I received from living at the monastery was the gift of no escape. Or I should say, the gift of dispelling the illusion that I could escape from myself.

In the world, I could get away with avoiding whatever threatened me. I could surround myself with what made me feel comfortable, safe, and secure. I never had to change or grow a whole lot, and certainly not in any significant way. I could always take a detour to what I liked and what I wanted.

In fact, setting up your life this way is seen as the ideal. Getting what you want is right. Right? Everybody else is doing it.

Conversely, the monastery was set up in a way that didn't take what I wanted into consideration *at all*. It loved me too much to let me settle for this.

In the beginning, I was given tasks like cleaning outhouses, prepping vegetables in the kitchen, or weeding in the garden. Then my work moved on to more complex tasks like handling power tools and driving the monastery vehicles. Then I was asked to supervise other people doing those cleaning tasks and crew-related work. Soon, threatening everything inside of me, I was asked to be responsible for an entire department – like being the cook, or the gardener, or running the online business. At one point, I was doing all three of these at once!

To bring on the sleepless nights, I was next asked to do the terrifying task of facilitating groups and offering one-on-one guidance appointments with people. These were perhaps the most intense experiences of all. The voices screamed, "You don't know how to do this!"

But what could I say? No was not an option.

The only response to any given task was either "yes" or "good-bye."

As a result of saying "yes," paying attention, dropping the stories and focusing instead on the tasks at hand, I received the greatest gift of all: learning to love learning. I reinvented myself into a man who could be ready for *anything* and avoided *nothing*.

I cooked for retreats with over 30 participants, I assisted with our projects in Africa, I built buildings, I created a cartoon series that taught people how suffering occurred in human beings and how to end it. I did things that really scared me. But they also excited me and pushed my limits.

I rose through the resistance because I was not permitted to indulge the crappy voice in my head that believed I couldn't do "something that was beyond me."

It's what I was learning since the first day I showed up at the monastery: Either go into the kitchen to chop carrots and be miserable or go into the kitchen to chop carrots and be happy. The choice was mine. I was going into the kitchen to chop carrots regardless.

WHAT IS SPIRITUAL PRACTICE?

The Great Way is not difficult
for those not attached to preferences.
When not attached to love or hate,
all is clear and undisguised.
Separate by the smallest amount, however,
and you are as far from it as heaven is from earth.
—Hsin Hsin Ming

Spiritual practice isn't about manipulating life experiences to get what you want.

There's nothing noble about sheltering yourself from the world. Or habitually responding with aversion and rejection. Or making your life small enough for comfort.

There's also nothing honorable about surrounding yourself with only the best, clinging to ease and gravitating toward what you love. That's just another attachment to preferences, the flip side of pushing away. One more tug in the perpetual tug-of-war with life.

The Buddha said suffering was wanting that which you don't have, wishing you didn't have what you do have, being around those you don't like, and prevented from being around those you do like.

I love this/I hate that. I want this/I don't want that. This is good/that is bad.

A never-ending world of suffering and dissatisfaction.

So, what is spiritual practice, then?

It is working out the puzzle within yourself. It's getting clear about the nature of the voices in your head, learning about the multiple aspects of yourself, finding your authentic self, and directing your attention to the wise, compassionate and conscious Inner Mentor within who can guide your life perfectly.

It is using everything in your life as a mirror to see how suffering is created and held in place. It is experiencing circumstances as spiritual opportunities to explore within yourself so your attachments, preferences, and suffering may be released.

Acknowledged, accepted, embraced, and let go.

When suffering is released, spiritual evolution and cultivation can begin. It's the birth of the creative force within you and around you.

It's when the real magic starts to happen. And you'd better buckle your seatbelt because it's going to be an incredible ride.

LOVE EVERYONE†

I fell in love with a fluffy white and black cat that wandered onto the monastery property. She was so beautiful. I took excellent care of her. I used to spend hours pulling the Velcro-like burrs that got stuck in her long fur when she came to visit my hermitage.

The monastery eventually decided she was better off living with a neighbor instead of us. That meant I would never see her again. When I heard the news, I became quite sad. The day she was picked up by her new owners and gone for good was one of the hardest days of my training.

That night, I sat in meditation. Tears were streaming down my cheeks. When the bell rang to finish my meditation, I asked a question, "How do you let go of someone you love?"

The answer that appeared was, "Love everyone."

I'll never forget the magnitude of that response. My heart opened up beyond its broken capacity to include all of those around me. The feeling was so overwhelming that it was impossible to experience loss.

Love everyone.

IS IT COMPASSIONATE?

I spent many years training to discover that compassion is an inside-out experience. Many of the things my teacher did to train the monks would not look compassionate to the outside world. Sometimes compassion would come in like a whisper and at other times it would come in like a roar.

First and foremost, compassion is a transformation of how an individual relates to her or himself. It requires some waking up.

While an action may appear to be "measurably" compassionate, one can never really tell. Because who is going to have the big picture perspective to know?

I'm not suggesting that we hold back from sharing generously, practicing inclusion, expressing kindness, or embracing understanding. It's just that those actions are a byproduct of an awakened heart.

SPIRITUAL LOVE NOTES (PART 1)

When I first arrived at the Zen monastery, I wanted to fit in. I tried to do my best. I wanted to be useful to everyone.

It's funny; looking back, I can see just how rampant my social conditioning was. The voices in my head were triggered left and right when new environments and unexpected situations threatened them. I later saw this behavior with all the new guests who showed up, too. There's nothing like being in a silent monastery where no one is talking to you to trigger all sorts of irrational thoughts!

"Do they like me?

"Was I supposed to do that?

"What will they think of me if I request that?

"How can I get approval now?"

My spiritual journey started when I discovered something was amiss with one of the benches on the monastery porch. My heart leapt. I happily saw my opportunity to be useful! With great smugness, I went into the dining hall, grabbed a big Sharpie marker and some paper, and I wrote my sign, "Do not sit on this bench." And I taped it to that bench so others could see it.

Every time I passed that bench during the day, I smiled because I heard in my head just how good I was. In my mind, I pictured the Guestmaster and my teacher nodding at me in approval, while I was glowing and smiling back. Spiritual brownie points were inevitably coming my way.

Later in the afternoon, I got a note addressed to me on the message board. I eagerly popped it open and read it.

> "Alex,
>
> Please do not make signs and tape them to things without communicating first.
>
> In lovingkindness,
> Guestmaster"

I was shocked.

If you were watching me read that note (something you weren't permitted to do at the monastery), you'd think it had said, "Alex, You're the biggest f*ing idiot on the planet. After lunch, we're going to take you out back behind the shed and shoot you. In lovingkindness, Guestmaster."

I couldn't believe it.

After the initial blow wore off, I felt hurt. Embarrassed. And then angry. Pissed off. The voices flared up and went into high gear.

"Well, why the hell didn't they tell me it wasn't an okay thing to do in the orientation? *They* put up signs all the time. How was I supposed to know? With the 1,001 guidelines they have, surely they could have added, 'Please do not put signs up on things without permission.'"

I walked around all day with a cloud of hatred covering me.

But when I reread the note later that night, it said only...

> "Alex,
>
> Please do not make signs and tape them to things without communicating first.
>
> In lovingkindness,
> Guestmaster"

...I noticed that it was written very matter-of-factly.

I scratched my head in disbelief.

Wow! What the heck was my intense reaction about? The voices in my head filled in the imaginary blanks, read between the lines and supplied the "true meaning."

I'm glad I kept the note. I had the impulse to crumple it up several times during the day, like it was some venomous animal or an offensive insult I wanted out of my sight and destroyed.

Later, when I eventually became the Guestmaster, I learned that all the notes were to be intentionally written in a neutral tone of voice because they were just "information." No judgment. No blame. Just the facts. Please do, or don't do, this.

This was the point of being at the monastery. To see through all of the beliefs, assumptions, and voices. To see how taking things personally caused me to suffer so I could end suffering. The notes were spiritual gifts to help me awaken.

This incident with the bench was my initiation to the message board and all the spiritual opportunities to come.

SPIRITUAL LOVE NOTES (PART 2)

I had a knack for finding things amiss. I thought it was only fitting that I put my keen skills of observation to work for me.

I had gotten the hang of receiving notes from the Guestmaster that were challenging for me to read, ego-crushing notes like "Alex, Please do not leave your shoes on the porch. Be sure to use the shoe rack instead. In lovingkindness, Guestmaster."

In a flash, I decided I would help the Guestmaster. "If you can't beat them, join them." I would catch anyone who was doing something wrong and then tip the Guestmaster off.

Curiously, it made me feel better about myself, or at least it lessened the sting of feeling bad about myself. If these notes were demolishing me, I could "spread the wealth" and be sure others felt this way, too. Goodness knows the Guestmaster only has one set of eyes. I could help him catch more lawbreaking monks and, in the process, take the focus off me.

I left notes like, "Guestmaster, John left his shoes on the porch instead of using the shoe rack. In lovingkindness, Alex" and "Guestmaster, Sophia didn't wash her hands before serving herself food. In lovingkindness, Alex" and "Guestmaster, Todd took an extra spoonful of almond butter at breakfast (the guideline is one). In lovingkindness, Alex."

Those notes would go up on the message board with a deep thrust of the pushpin. A jab that, if it had words, would have said, "Got you, sucker!"

Well, funny enough, I didn't get the appreciation I was expecting. The note I pulled down off the message board for "Alex" one morning didn't say, "Alex, We noticed your great skills of observation and we didn't want them to go to waste. Please take over the role of Guestmaster starting today. In lovingkindness, Work Director."

Instead, it said, "Alex, Over the past three days you have left the lights on in the kitchen after being the last one to leave, burned the beans for lunch today, and forgot to record group discussion the other night. Please pay attention to what you are doing instead of pointing out what others are doing wrong. In lovingkindness, Guestmaster."

No matter how many times I received notes from that message board, I still reacted. I still managed to be shocked, hurt, defensive and then angry, in that order. I knew that the monastery was bashing the ego and supporting my heart, but I still read those notes as though they were bashing me. I took them personally. I identified with the voices of egocentricity.

Only when I finally did take on the Guestmaster role was I able to see the immense amount of compassion expressed in those notes. Each one held up a mirror to the recipient with an opportunity to "wake up," a chance to receive the note as a helpful reminder, a moment to say, "Thank you."

SPIRITUAL LOVE NOTES (PART 3)

The note was back in my hand again.

I had been trying to post it on the message board repeatedly throughout the day. At breakfast. At lunch. After working meditation. And now during snack.

But I couldn't do it. The voice in my head said, "You're a bad monk, and everyone will find out." This is the one that did me in every time.

So now what was I going to do? Read it again for the umpteenth time? What will I erase now? How will I rephrase my note?

To receive the toiletries and clothes we needed, we were asked to leave a note for the Guestmaster making a request. This was so the Guestmaster could get guidance on the approval of our requests. Once the items were approved, they would then be added to the weekly errands run.

To me, this whole procedure was torture. I wanted to be a "good monk." In my mind, a "good monk" should pretty much have no needs whatsoever. So, the fact that my note had more than one item on it was already problematic.

In my imagination, I saw the Guestmaster and my teacher meeting over tea in the Work Director's office scratching their heads and puzzling over the pettiness of my stupid requests. "Toothpaste and socks?! Doesn't he know that when I was training in the monastery with my teacher, I walked barefoot in the snow?"

My stomach knotted. Could I wait another week without warm socks? This was ridiculous! What was I trying to prove?

I gathered my courage and posted that damn note back up on the message board. Then I looked around to see if anyone was watching before scurrying back to my meal.

And then I heard the voices in my head launch into me again.

"You're so needy and weak.

"They're going to find out what you need and then they're going to withhold them all from you intentionally. Why are you giving them the upper hand over you?

"Can't you wait another week without warm socks?"

I sat there and breathed with a scowl on my face. I did everything I could to let those crappy voices go. Every time I saw the Guestmaster get up from her meal, I rose in the direction of the message board. When I caught myself, I sat back down and stuffed more soup into my mouth.

Then I heard the ping-pong retort, "This is so silly. It's only a stupid errands note. Why are you making such a big deal out of this? A 'good monk' wouldn't be so self-centered..."

Finally, the Guestmaster collected the notes while I was washing dishes in the kitchen. I heard the voices say, "You're a bad monk and everyone will find out." But it was too late this time. The Guestmaster had my note in her pile. I could finally breathe. It was officially out of my hands and out of my power.

Which was a perfect metaphor for my training. In this way, the message board became my formidable spiritual teacher in the art of facing resistance and letting go.

I repeatedly practiced posting notes and walking away despite the cries from the voices. I left my results to the Universe (in the form of the Guestmaster). "Yes" or "no" was beyond my control. My job was to show up, take action, and walk away.

That felt really good after a while. Seeing the resistance and choosing to take the first step anyway became empowering. I did this in other activities, like facilitating groups, offering guidance appointments, or creating curriculum for retreats.

The message board was my spiritual teacher.

The funny part is that most of the time my requests were accepted. At one point I was so confident that I started requesting some rather exotic supplements that were promptly rejected. But by then, I was well beyond my attachment to "yes" or fear of "no." I wasn't concerned about what a "good" or a "bad" monk was.

I was free.

THE VOICES ADORE A VACUUM

Why are transitions so challenging? Why is there such a massive dip in your energy system after you accomplish a goal? When you finish a project or when you're leaving a retreat, you suddenly feel different. Have you noticed this?

You were on a high. Your mood and enthusiasm were building all along. You were in the flow. You had your focus and attention so captivated that there was no room for it to be anywhere else. Then, as you're cleaning up, packing things away, and moving on, you notice that familiar "empty feeling."

Perhaps there's a review of how it went going on in your head. Or you're just wandering around now with no direction. Maybe you're sharing your enthusiasm with people who were not involved, and they just don't get it.

Suddenly, somewhat alarmingly, all the good feelings you had are gone. Down the drain and wiped out. Like nothing ever happened.

In an attempt to escape this void, you compulsively go looking for some familiar coping behavior, whatever that is for you. Perhaps it's shopping for stuff, eating fast food, drinking alcohol, talking non-stop, surfing the web, getting lost on social media. Whatever.

Unfortunately, what you use to fill the gap will typically result in you getting a beating from the voices. Then you end up feeling horrible. Much worse than before.

Interestingly enough, the gap, or the void, is not inherently a negative emptiness. In fact, it's a place that is pregnant with possibilities. From the emptiness, everything arises.

However, we don't see the process the voices have been setting us up for since the beginning. With all that lovely energy, they are just waiting for an opening to insert themselves into it so they can hijack our attention when we are not consciously directing it. And then we get lost in the habitual, suffering conversation, which is precisely where the voices like to take us.

When I'm coaching my clients through their big projects and goals, I always like to prepare them for "the day after," the moment when all their upbeat energy could get robbed. I do the same thing to help my retreatants as they're leaving to go back out into the world.

First, I warn them there will likely be the temptation to engage in some coping behavior as they transition. I ask them to identify it. If they abandon themselves by talking someone's ear off, or eating junk food, to jot that down in their journal. I tell them they're going to need to look out for those behaviors.

I then ask them what they think would support their hearts instead. Then we start listing ways they might care for themselves. I'll ask them to call out some ideas.

"A walk in nature."

"Prepare a healthy meal."

"Some time in silence."

"Take a nice, long hot bath."

"Acknowledge myself for the good work I've done."

I write what they're brainstorming on the whiteboard until we have a pretty impressive list of alternatives they could use to support themselves. Now they're armed with Plan B.

I always make sure to underline the fact that *if*, on the off chance, they fall for one of their coping behaviors, despite this proper preparation, to please indulge no beatings from the voices whatsoever. I tell them that it's a moment to bow to the voices, that they may have won this match but not the entire game.

Then I ask them to recommit by practicing being kinder to themselves than they think they should be. They have the opportunity to fill the gap with compassion every time the voices fill the gap with suffering, so transitions become a time of nurturing and acknowledgment, rather than a time of feeling bad.

117

KEEPING COMMITMENTS

I talk a lot about the importance of keeping commitments when it comes to maintaining a meditation practice – to make an agreement with yourself to sit for a particular length of time, to put it on your schedule, and then to actually do it.

Because the voices of resistance will take a practice such as meditation and begin to fabricate their own "rules" about how to do it, creating agreements makes sense.

The voices are always on the lookout for "better ideas" to thwart us. They'll insist, "Don't keep your hands like that. That's too uncomfortable." Or, "You were told to do it sitting up, but lying down would feel so much better." Or, "The instructor said that five minutes was plenty, but you know an hour would be impressive!" The next thing you know, meditation may not even resemble the meditation practice you were taught, or it becomes this Herculean contest you must endure to meet some nebulous standard.

When you don't do it, what will the voices say? "This meditation thing just doesn't work. It's too hard. You're not cut out for this!"

And you end up quitting.

The voices can rack up meditation as just one more thing you've failed at. How self-serving, since meditation ferrets out the voices and exposes them so you can see what they are, what they do and how they work.

Keep your commitments, even if you need to consciously re-commit later on. Start with less to ensure you're successful. Then compassionately agree to renegotiate a new commitment. Take your practice out of the hands of the voices and back into your own. This begins the process of taking back your life and putting you back into the driver's seat.

WHAT OR HOW?

If you are the master, the mind follows you like a shadow. If you are not a master, you have to follow the mind like a shadow.
—Osho

In 2016, I met with a startup entrepreneur in a downtown Boulder cafe. She and her partner had developed an idea for an app that helped people intentionally lock their mobile devices from use. It was designed to help reduce the temptation to excessively use their devices out of habit. She asked to meet with me because she had heard of my background in Zen, mindfulness, and meditation. While we sat there in the cafe, she told me how this idea had originated.

Her young nephew was a happy-go-lucky kid who played outdoors and was full of life – until he was given a tablet as a gift. After that, he turned into an addicted, mobile device zombie. He never left the house and his entire demeanor changed. He was shut down, pale, and glued to playing games on his tablet during all of his free time. She'd seen this same phenomenon happen to others in her life, including herself. This stark transformation right before her eyes was the catalyst that sparked her to develop and release her app.

She asked me if I had any thoughts about our modern dilemma of device addiction. She wanted to see if my insights could help her give validity to her app marketing message. I told her I truly admired her work and her sincere passion to help people. Those who could benefit from using this app would certainly find it tremendously life-changing.

But I told her truthfully the issue was deeper than merely device addiction. I'd seen how addiction worked in my own life. I told her how I, and other people, turned to the content of our problems to blame. Whether that be money, television, shopping, or even our own minds. It was too easy to say that the mobile devices were to blame.

It was our *relationship* to these things that was the true issue. It wasn't the *what*, the tablet, but rather the *how*, how he related to the tablet.

Our teacher at the monastery repeatedly reminded the senior monks about having a proper relationship to our computers. We had access to them because they assisted us with our work. They were not toys. They were tools to help us get our jobs done. She was very clear. Her insistence was a powerful example of what compassionate communication and support looked like.

I've seen people blame money as their problem – "the root of all evil." I've seen people blame their minds. Their minds are scattered. Money is intrinsically neutral. Our minds are like clear glasses of water. It's what we do with them that causes either freedom or suffering.

In this world, it's extremely popular to point fingers at what's causing our unhappiness. To assume that we are helpless. To assume that the fault lies outside of us. Training people to create a better relationship with themselves, where they commit to guidelines and compassionate self-mentoring, will always be more effective than adopting a victim stance where things, people, or outside circumstances are to blame.

TAKING THE WHEEL

Just because our relationship with the content of life is what the focus of practice is all about, *the how* and not *the what*, that doesn't mean we turn our practice over to the voices in our heads for guidance regarding *the what*.

The voices will look at an alcoholic's addiction to alcohol, say to him that if he were truly and sincerely doing mindfulness practice, he'd be able to spend the night in a bar and not drink. That it's his relationship to alcohol that is the problem. Not the alcohol.

Well, this is just nonsense and a set up for a beating.

He needs help.

The voices like to make life into a competition so we can fail. And when we fail, they swoop in to make us feel bad. They will stop us from doing what will support us and encourage us to do what will harm us. They will do that our whole life long, if we allow them to.

If we don't address the voices now, we will hear their last and final beating when we get to our deathbeds. The voices will fill us with so much regret and blame about how we played so small and made such bad decisions. They will attempt to completely wipe away whatever good we did in the world by making the last word a bad one and our entire life a failure.

If we let them.

A TRUSTWORTHY FRIEND[*]

Can you be trusted with this one precious life you have been given? Can you find your Inner Mentor, who will help you make conscious choices – decisions made from acceptance and compassion? Will you pick this good friend instead of the anti-coach who jumps in to sabotage your life?

We must take our lives back from the voices.

We must keep our agreements with ourselves because what we are doing is building trust within ourselves.

And before you can trust yourself, you must become trustworthy.

Imagine that you have a friend you're counting on to show up for you. When the time comes, your friend doesn't show up. You ask that friend to show up for you again. Once again, that friend fails to show up.

What will happen?

You will stop trusting that friend! Your "friend" can't be counted on!

It's the same with you.

This lack of integrity is the reason most of us have a jaded relationship with ourselves. We've let ourselves down so many times that we can't count on ourselves anymore.

We are continually abandoning ourselves when we follow the voices in our heads. They talk us into unhelpful activities and behaviors. When they're not doing that, they're talking us into ignoring the beneficial behaviors we've agreed to.

After a time, we begin to lose faith that anything will ever make a difference for us, or that we'll ever change for the better, because we have given up on ourselves so quickly and consistently. We eventually say to ourselves, "Why bother?"

Every time we fail to keep our commitments, we become more and more untrustworthy with our lives.

I'm telling you this not because I want you to feel bad about it. That would just put this insight back into the hands of the voices to abuse you. I'm sharing this because it's good to take note of how this works so you can start the process of turning it around.

How is that done?

The first step is to learn how to direct your attention. Learning to direct your attention is a process. It's something most of us have never really been taught how to do. It's the beginning stage of becoming your own best friend. To keep your attention with yourself instead of the voices.

When your attention is with you, you can then learn to practice self-mentoring. Self-mentoring is learning to see yourself as a person who is perfect just the way you are. From a place of wholeness, you can then assist yourself to become whomever you want to be.

There is a deep and satisfying pleasure that comes from starting from a place of perfection rather than seeing yourself as damaged or broken. Or someone who needs to be healed first.

It's empowering and life-affirming.

From this confident stance, you approach Life and ask it, "What can I offer you? What have I been given and how can I give that back? What am I compelled to give that would be of service to you? What would be selfish of me not to give?"

Once you discover the answers to these questions, then ask yourself, "How can I support myself to accomplish this? How can I take this mission out of the hands of resistance and apply it, bit by bit, with kindness and compassion?"

Begin with these simple steps.

Over time, you will start to train yourself to become more trustworthy. You will replace what is not helpful to you with what is vital. What is mean and cruel with what is supportive and encouraging. What is isolating with what is connecting. Poisonous with life-giving, self-hatred with compassion.

Best of all, you will gain a true friend who is trustworthy. *You!*

YOU COUNT[*]

Receive a guest with the same attitude you have when alone. When alone, maintain the same attitude you have in receiving guests.
—Soyen Shaku

In the teachings of the Buddha, there are such astonishing assertions like "There is no self and other," and "Everything is one."

Years ago, I had the opportunity to see this lesson for myself at the monastery. Tired from a day's work, I would go home and face my uninsulated plywood hermitage in 20-degree weather. I did not have an ounce of energy left in me to start a fire in the stove.

The voices would say, "It's only for you, and you really don't feel like it."

Years later, I was blessed with the opportunity to care for a big, beautiful German Shepherd.

Now that I had him to care for, I somehow discovered the miraculous willingness to start fires in my hermitage. Of course, I enjoyed them too.

Somehow, I mustered up the energy to do this consistently. For him.

Alone, I didn't matter. But because of him, it was okay to make an effort.

This process sometimes showed up after leaving the monastery, when I thought it would be fun to cook something new for myself. Since I would be preparing food for myself, I'd hear the same voice say, "It's only for you. Why go through all that work?"

It still takes a lot of self-mentoring to break through the self-hatred. To practice seeing myself as "a someone," worthy of kindness and compassion. To take a stand against the dismissive voice and say, "Yes, in fact, I do matter!"

That's the lesson I have been learning, one that I hope you take to heart as well. Only when you get that you matter can you live as though what you do matters. So participate. Even if you're the only one who shows up.

In the end, you're all you've really got.

You are counting on you.

THERE IS NO BALANCE

One of the most popular questions I regularly receive from clients and students is, "What is the balance between 'just letting things be and going with the flow' versus 'working hard to make stuff happen'?"

My response is, "There is no balance."

I explain by describing the following:

Both are important, all the time. You must accept Life and Now as perfect exactly the way they are *and* do everything you can to grow, develop, evolve and make a difference for the sake of Life. They are one song.

Here's where we get into trouble:

The voices take "acceptance" and define it as "resignation, being nice, being passive, spacing out, being a doormat, and condoning." So, I run into people on this side of the duality who are sitting in their rooms "manifesting" what they want by doing nothing. They're just waiting for the good stuff to fall into their laps. Or they're proudly saying things like, "Well, if it were meant to happen, it would have happened by now. It must be a sign from the Universe that..."

In my experience, it's a very easy way to remain a victim of what happens to you in life.

On the flipside, the voices take "effort" and define it as "racing to the top, me first, no pain no gain, and looking out for #1." People over here are overworked, beaten bloody, see themselves as lazy if they take a moment off. They're competitive, on the verge of burnout, and overcommitted. Families fall apart, and areas of their lives falter due to lack of attention.

We can vacillate between these two.

If wandering around as the "happy-go-lucky" person doesn't work, we can become triggered to get serious and transform into "the go-getter."

The same is true the other way around. In fact, I meet many corporate leaders who think the answer is to do what they love (like become a yoga teacher). From "go-getter" to "happy-go-lucky." That must be the answer.

But a duality swing is still a duality swing and, in my experience, you're fooling yourself if you think that one equals happiness and the other doesn't.

That said, in and of themselves, there's nothing wrong with either of them.

Happy-go-lucky is perfect to go on a hike with, but horrible if you put this person in charge of your credit cards.

The go-getter is excellent to oversee your business, but horrible when you bring this person out on a date.

The real issue is that there's no one in charge of seeing who's appropriate to arise at any given moment. No leader asking, "Who is the best person for the job?" So, the voices jump in to fill the vacuum (and make a mess of everything).

You want to learn how to be the compassionate Inner Mentor, the one who can look at you and say, "I love you exactly as you are and I'll help you become any way you want to be."

When all the parts of you *and* your mentor are reunited, you'll be making beautiful music together in no time.

THE SPIRITUAL MERITS
OF DOING THE OPPOSITE

George Costanza, a character from the TV series *Seinfeld*, made this practice famous when he declared out loud that "Nothing in my life has ever worked as planned. Every instinct I've ever had has been wrong. So from now on, I'm going to do the opposite." When he did, starting with the typical lunch he had, everything in his life began to work miraculously. He was kind and polite when he wanted to blow up, and he blew up when he tried to shirk away. He practiced restraint when he would want to act, and acted when he would typically restrain. He spoke his mind when he would generally please and was pleasing when he would habitually give others a piece of his mind!

So, let's take a look at why this actually makes sense as a legitimate practice.

Following on the premise that the voices in our heads talk us into doing what is unhelpful and talk us out of doing what is helpful, it would seem that practicing doing the opposite has the potential to foil the voices and ultimately free us.

Because of our social conditioning, we have predisposed survival strategies in place to keep risk, danger, discomfort, unpleasantness, and change from happening to us. This strategy is why certain groups of people will avoid going out and prefer to be alone (called introverts), and other groups of people will avoid being alone with themselves in preference to being out with others all the time (called extroverts).

Both strategies have benefits and liabilities. Neither approach, I would argue, really applies to either group exclusively since there are times when introverts are extroverts and extroverts are introverts. It's just that certain parts of us have gotten more airtime and support than others, so they feel like they're "really us" most of the time.

At the Zen monastery, we knew this conditioning was true on many levels. Therefore, we wouldn't ask new monks what they were good at or what skills they could offer the monastery. Instead, they would be tossed out to face the voices in their heads shrieking while doing an unfamiliar task. They would be shown, step-by-step, the exact process required to do that task. And they would follow the instructions precisely with a beginner's mind.

Did terror arise? Certainly! As did the excitement of unknown adventures.

You've noticed this too. Because no matter how hard we may try to avoid it, change does happen. Whenever I've moved to a new location, I'd notice my wide-eyed enthusiasm would begin to build.

I'd be discovering new walking paths, new groups of people to meet, unique shops to visit, and new opportunities to face. But over the coming days, weeks and months those paths would become well worn. The people become cliques, the shops become the same, and I wouldn't see much available to me outside of what I was currently doing.

There's science to prove that we have parts of our brains that prefer to be on autopilot. These are the parts that corner us into the status quo. While we may say we want something different, we are constrained to stay the same.

At the monastery, it was simple. We either said "yes" to what we were asked to do or we said "goodbye." When my teacher was finally admitted into the monastery where she trained, she told us that her Roshi promised her he would find everything she disliked and "push her nose into it." Just like my teacher, I was at the monastery to face down the voices and free myself from the limitations that enslaved me. To see what life was like outside of what I preferred, what I liked, what I wanted, what I felt comfortable with, and what I believed was true about me.

Out in the world, it was easy to abandon myself. If I became uncomfortable with someone or a situation I was in, I could leave. Instead of learning something, I could ask my buddy who was good at it to do it for me. Instead of facing my fears, I could avoid them.

Even today, when I'm working with my clients, I know resistance is a good sign. It means they're going up against change. They're surprised at my excitement, mostly because they're interpreting the resistance as a bad sign. But again, remember *The Opposite.*

If you're experiencing resistance, it only means you're on the path to more growth. It's not supposed to be easy.

Nothing significant for you ever has been.

WILLINGNESS IS SHOWING UP

There is no such thing as great teachers. Only great students.

Of course, teachers can evoke a great student from an average student. In fact, that is a teacher's job. What ultimately makes for a compelling teacher-student relationship is the student's willingness to show up. That is the primary requirement. A student is to meet the teacher halfway. It's what I mean when I use the expression, "Show up for yourself."

Whether you accept me as your teacher or not, I am asking you to show up as you read this book. I'm asking you to read these stories and lessons to see how the principles in them apply to your life.

When you show up for yourself, you are willing to stay open and stick with it. You're eager to see the lesson in every situation and use it to your benefit. You will fall, brush yourself off, understand why you fell, and then keep going. By doing so, you will have learned something.

Fall down seven times.
Stand up eight.
—Japanese proverb

We all love students who fall but get up, don't we? A spirit like this is the epitome of heroism in action.

I've had students in my online retreats whose participation I enjoyed immensely. Every day, I looked forward to reading their reports. Here's how they showed up:

- They did the assignments.
- They paid attention to what arose for them while doing the assignments.
- They shared their insights with everyone else afterward.
- They did this consistently.

Sometimes they would miss a day or two. But then they would bounce right back to tell us how they found themselves missing a day or two.

"It was those voices of resistance!" they would say.

A smile would cross my face after reading their experience, because the missing day provided them with a powerful insight. To this I always reply, "Excellent! Good for you!"

Here's my confession: I enjoy showing up for these types of students. I do my darndest to pull down the sun, moon, and stars for them. Nothing lights me up more than those who show up for themselves with willingness.

You've seen people like this before, too. They're the ones who take notes, remain curious, and use everything as an opportunity to learn something. Contrast this with people who do the bare minimum, say nothing works, pretend to know everything and complain about how circumstances aren't right.

The question will eventually arise, "Shouldn't we be compassionate to these people too?"

Yes, of course.

The best way I have found is to be a compassionate mirror. To show them how they are choosing not to show up for themselves. To evoke the part of them who, in fact, will show up for themselves.

It is ultimately up to them. You can't do the work for them. You can't drag people to salvation. It must be their choice. They must choose authenticity instead of the voices. The ball is on their side of the court.

I'll never forget, at the end of one of our precepts ceremonies at the monastery, a newly precepted monk waited for our teacher to put the rosaries around his neck. Instead, my teacher just held the rosaries out to him. She told him he must take them and put them around his own neck. The spiritual responsibility was his and his alone.

Over the years, I have used willingness as a gauge to see if people are ready to do the work of ending suffering and transform their lives. I can never, ever want it more for others than they want it for themselves.

The Buddha himself said, *"You must work out your own salvation diligently."*

You must work it out. You must want it. And wanting it doesn't show up in words.

It shows up in you showing up.

READY WHEN READY

 senior monk at the monastery once said that he recited something to himself before each group he facilitated:

May all who wish for freedom find it. Wherever illusion is a guardian and a barricade, let it remain.

I adopted his recitation and here is what it came to mean for me: I will do my best to help people end suffering and become free. However, if they are not ready to do this work and choose the voices as their authorities, I will let them go.

As a coach, I hear excuses made by the voices all the time. "I'm too busy. I don't have enough money; I can't do this; I don't have enough time; I don't feel like it; it's too hard; I'll do it later..."

What I've also seen is those who say "no" to support choose the same resistance that causes them to flounder about in life. It saddens my heart because really good people are stuck underneath all these bad decisions and lose. The voices win the day.

We must let go of our attachment to the outcome regardless of how painful it is to sit and watch someone continually and repeatedly choose resistance. We can't force them to accept their hearts.

I ran into a former client in my neighborhood while we were both out walking our dogs. She told me she was trying to convince an acquaintance of hers to sign up to do the online retreat I offer. It made me laugh, and then made her laugh because we both saw how resistance was working to keep her friend from doing what would help her. "Isn't it frustrating? You can totally see how it would change her entire life if she did it, right? But she won't."

Yup, lots of head nodding. An inside "joke" among those of us who have worked to free ourselves from the voices. We know what those voices will do to stop us from succeeding.

The conclusion I have drawn is this: Let them go. They'll be ready when they're ready. They either need that intelligent "ah ha" moment when the choice is obvious, or they need to suffer a bit more before they will do what will help them. Either way, saving others isn't our responsibility.

It's theirs.

RELATIONSHIPS ARE
LIKE THE ROOF OF A HOUSE

The way I am in a relationship with another is one side of the roof, and the way the other is being in a relationship with me is the flip side of our roof. Together, we meet at the apex and we "hold each other up." The roof is our relationship. It's a structure held in place by how each of us is being.

I tell my clients that when you stop holding up the roof the way you've been doing it, the roof will do one of two things: Either it will collapse or what needs to hold it in place will shift. That is, we won't be together anymore, or the new way I am being will call forth a complementary way of being from the other person.

For example, if I continue to play the victim and you play the rescuer, I will continuously call forth from you the rescuer. Together, that's our roof. Nothing will change until there's no need to play our victim/rescuer roles. Either of us can shift. Either I take charge of my life and have no need for rescuing or my rescuing partner stops coming in to save me, leaving me to find my adequacy.

It's uncomfortable to shift because that's how we find each

other in our relationships in the first place. It can be hard to change because your partner may not be interested in the dynamic between you changing. They risk losing their entire identity. They might be just fine with the situation, especially when changing it would be a significant inconvenience to them.

I had a client once who would always remind her husband of all the important things he needed to remember to do. She decided to stop doing that because it was energetically taxing her. When he needed to remember to drive out to an event he was to attend, it was for him to remember. It freed up a lot of energy for her and empowered her husband to be more responsible with his own life. Sure, it was uncomfortable for both of them. She felt bad for "not being a good wife" or for no longer pleasing him with such a minor thing, and he felt angry that "he had one more thing on his plate to track and had to keep a schedule with alarms to remind himself of his appointments." The voices between them would try to pull them back to the way it was by pointing out how "they used to be such a good team."

But they failed to notice they were a rather dysfunctional team! She was overwhelmed and enabling while he was enabled and dependent.

It takes some growing up to shift the roof so we are each supporting each other to be the best we can. To see the other person's adequacy and call forth from them their powerful self.

PEOPLE WHO
HAVE BEEN HURT IN LOVE

People have been hurt so much that they no longer open themselves up to the possibility of love. They're trying to protect themselves from being injured.

Look, the bad story that's harming you over and over again is inside of you. Meanwhile, you're driving out all potential of love. For what? A story about how you're so wounded? So what now? Are you going to continue punishing yourself and denying us the pleasure of your company because you *might* get hurt again? Are you going to do this into perpetuity? Are you some weakling who has no life at all and others have all the power over you?

Or are you failing to see the true story? That you're adequate to your life experience. That you are more than able to stand up and create the circumstances you want. To build the life you want. To be the powerful creator and experience happiness. To claim your birthright.

HOW TO TAKE RESPONSIBILITY

When you take responsibility for your own life experience and stop blaming others for your dissatisfaction, you become a social relief.

When you take your satisfaction into your own hands, people can breathe easier while they're around you.

Why?

Because you're not attempting to get your unmet needs met by them. You're not a burden. You're not demanding love or expecting them to fulfill you. You're not some poor unfortunate soul waiting for others to come around and rescue you or make you whole.

You're whole because you experience yourself as whole.

Not only are you whole, but you're a bottomless source of conscious, compassionate awareness. You have so much love inside that you're actually an overflowing of happiness.

Your happiness doesn't belong to your friends, parents, partners, kids or anyone else on this planet. They don't have it. They haven't got a clue what that even looks like. As a matter of fact, the only thing that's likely on their minds is how they're going to get happiness *from you!*

It's up to you to break the expectation for happiness to come from the outside.

Because in truth, happiness, love, and satisfaction have always been your responsibility. It's been yours all along. You're in charge.

What a relief!

THE PERSON
AND THE BEHAVIOR[†]

Imagine a dot on a whiteboard.

That's who you are. The dot represents authenticity. Everyone, deep down, wants the same thing. To be okay, to do the best they can, to be accepted, to get attention, to survive, and to make some contribution.

I seriously doubt many people wake up in the morning and say to themselves "I wonder how I can royally screw something up today," or "I wonder how I can have as many people as possible hate me."

Yet it's surprising how most of us treat others, and ourselves, on the assumption that these are our motives, that we are all intrinsically bad.

Now imagine a circle drawn around this dot. This circle represents our conditioned behaviors. These behaviors run the gamut of what human beings are capable of expressing, from the most atrocious acts of cruelty to the most inspiring acts of kindness.

They encompass the varying degrees of everything we like and dislike about others and ourselves.

What I have learned is that we confuse people's conditioned behaviors with who they are. We say "I hate criminals," or "I can't stand my husband," or "My kids drive me crazy."

I would argue that more accurate statements are "I hate the crimes that people commit," and "I can't stand it when my husband leaves his socks in the sink," and "It annoys me when my children ask me questions all day long."

If we could step back, remove ourselves from the stance of "the other as the enemy" and see their behaviors as the issue, then we have an opportunity to do something about addressing those behaviors directly.

At the end of the day, when you look into another person's eyes you see their humanity – something we all share in common. Our struggles and our victories, our joys and our sorrows. While certain behaviors are unacceptable, you as a human being are 100% acceptable.

When we can tease out "the behavior" from "the person," now we can do something. The person is not at fault or attacked. The person is okay.

What they're doing is not okay, but we can address those actions.

The point is never to confuse the person and his or her conditioned behaviors – the inside versus the outside.

WHY YOU SHOULD
NEVER FORGIVE YOURSELF

Forgiveness, by its very nature, implies that there's a "correct, better, good" way something could have gone and a "wrong, worse, bad" way it could have gone. And that someone – someone superior to another person – knows which way is which. And when the inferior person messes up, he or she needs to apologize to receive forgiveness from said superior person.

Inside of you, you must question: Who or what would get itself entangled in the whole fault, blame, right/wrong, feeling lousy drama?

If you look below the surface, you'll see that you are not always acting upon your own better judgment or volition. Often, you'll be set up by the voices in your head to do something unfortunate or unskillful. They'll talk you into eating the chocolate cake during your diet, skipping out on yoga to sleep in, or yelling at your poor husband instead of breathing and talking to him like an adult. Yes, the cake, sleep, and tantrum may feel good at the moment, but they'll come with a beating later. "Look at you! You have no will-power! What a loser you are!" Then the cycle will repeat.

If you look at this cycle, you'll see that you're the hapless pawn in the middle.

You only did what you were told to do (by the voices) and then got walloped for doing it (by the voices). The voices set you up and then knock you down. A complete one-two punch.

The real problem in this scenario is that you're listening to and believing the voices. Your responsibility is to practice consciously shining the light of awareness on those voices, so you stop falling for them.

I'm not abdicating you from responsibility, allowing you to say "the voices made me do it." In fact, I'm demanding you take respon-sibility to see through how this works. I'm demanding that you refuse to fall for the blame, shame, feel-bad game that comes with forgiveness.

So you see, you're not the one doing this to yourself. Why would you?

Therefore, why would you need to forgive yourself for your actions?

A better practice than self-forgiveness is to learn how you get duped by the voices in your head in the first place. Discover what they said to you that tricked you into believing them. Capture their language. See how you can help yourself. Resolve to make this challenge your spiritual practice.

Move away from finger-pointing and into action taking. Do what can make a difference.

When the voices try to talk you into your coping behavior, how can you help yourself compassionately? What can you do before, during and afterward? How can you set your life up to be successful?

Just as you don't need any forgiveness, you don't need to apologize either. In fact, the best "apology" is to vow never to let it happen again. If we're honest with ourselves, we'll see that we apologize to "feel better," not because we ever intend to do better. We apologize to "get off the hook" so we can continue to do the same behavior again in the future just so we can apologize again and again. Have you noticed?

Step in to break the voices' involvement in your feel-bad drama. Cut to the chase. Deal with them instead of focusing on what doesn't help. This isn't a call to excuse your own actions by blaming the voices. It's an opportunity to stop engaging with them and to live consciously outside of right/wrong and good/bad.

Free yourself from the blame that self-forgiveness brings and commit to changing once and for all – with mindfulness and compassionate self-mentoring.

A client once confessed to me that she didn't trust her fiancé. She told me she was having a hard time trusting him based on what he'd done in the past and her childhood traumas.

I told her that's fine. Give up on trusting. Just forget about it. Trust is pointless.

After some silence, she told me she was a little confused. She thought I was going to help her find a way to trust him. To tackle the voices in her head to see that she can lighten up a little.

I said, "Trust is overrated. When people say they want to trust, they mean they want to fall asleep and stop paying attention. They want to go on autopilot and move along through life blindly. It's the ostrich approach to life. It's a lot like 'hope' or 'belief.' I'm a big advocate for being super-awake and hyper-alert. I want you to be present with your fiancé. I want you to be with who he is being right now. Be with who *you* are being right now. Not drawing from the past, but rather, *right now*. If there's cause for concern, inquire in the most innocent way possible. Draw him out with curiosity and base your information on the facts rather than fictitious fantasies and delusions."

DON'T TRY TO CHANGE PEOPLE

Be not angry that you cannot make others as you wish them to be,
since you cannot make yourself as you wish to be.
—*Thomas à Kempis*

People have been trying to change each other since before the beginning of beginningless time.

It's so tiring. So intrusive. So counter-productive. So manipulative.

So easy.

The difficulty is simply sitting with our uncontrollable desire to get involved. With the need to rescue or the need to relieve pain. Or fix. Or eliminate. Never realizing that what others may need to express is exactly what needs to be expressed.

No matter how difficult that may be for us to witness.

If we were to be honest with ourselves, we'd realize that trying to change others is rarely for the benefit of the other person. We do it so we don't have to feel uncomfortable with ourselves and our own thoughts, so we can shut off their screaming and appease our ego.

No one ever sits with themselves or others. No one ever trusts each other's adequacy.

We look out and see others who are so frail and weak. We think they need to be spared their grief.

How arrogant. How self-centered.

The world doesn't need another screwed up person trying to save it. Please tend to your own life. Work out your own salvation diligently. Focus on your internal garden.

Let the fruit of your cultivation bring peace to the world.

Let inner peace create world peace.

STOP BLAMING THE VOICES

The devil made me do it.
— *Flip Wilson*

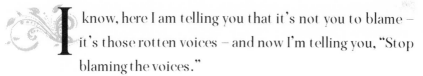 know, here I am telling you that it's not you to blame –
it's those rotten voices – and now I'm telling you, "Stop
blaming the voices."

So what gives?

For a long period of time at the monastery, group discussions
were filled with monks, neighbors and retreatants coming in to
blame the voices. We would tell the facilitator about how we had
been duped by those voices and we spared no detail in describing
how it happened. It was like going to a confessional and hearing
how the devil talked us into doing this or stopped us from doing
that. There was almost a certain level of pride in our ability to give
the blow-by-blow recounting of how the voices won. By the end of
the discussion, I remember leaving with a yucky, depleted feeling.

Until one day when our teacher brought us in to tell us the point of practice wasn't to listen to the voices, believe them, act on them, and then share how we had been victims to their influence. On the contrary. Our responsibility was to become aware of them and stop believing them. We had to stop acting on them.

The practice wasn't to indulge suffering – it was to end it!

So, while we weren't responsible for our thoughts (they seemed to happen of their own accord and out of our control), the place where we *did* have the power was in our ability to direct our attention and consciously choose how to respond.

This was why we were practicing.

You see, we are the ones with the bodies. The voices are not real. We don't need to be afraid of the voices (even though we act afraid most of the time – as though they pose a real threat). We need to take back our lives and stop making choices that lead to suffering.

Eventually, once you see how they work, you really need to stop it.

Part of my job description as a guide is to take a stand for you and your heart. I'm on your side and I'm against the voices. I will do whatever I can to free you from them. I play the role of the compassionate Inner Mentor. I model for you how that's done.

At some point, you will need to choose your Inner Mentor over the voices. Remember, your power is in your ability to direct your attention and choose. If you continue to choose the voices over the Inner Mentor, you will ultimately give your power away.

Instead, keep your power on what supports you.

SOMETIMES KICKING PEOPLE OUT IS THE MOST COMPASSIONATE THING TO DO

In spiritual practice, the student is never right.

If what you've been doing your whole life isn't working, it's a disservice to allow you to continue doing it. If you insist on complaining non-stop, being habitually late, or causing a disturbance to yourself or others, it needs to be addressed. The goal is to end suffering, not indulge it.

If it is permitted to go on, it is a dishonor to the God within you.

The spiritual teacher or master needs to point out to you what you're doing by any and all means necessary. Sometimes it's with a note. Sometimes it's with a guidance appointment. Sometimes it's with consequences.

Until you wake up. Or don't.

When I'm working with students and the teachings are not received, or the support falls on deaf ears, or they choose resistance instead of love, it's time to let them go. Indulging the behavior is unkind. It is unkind to reward them for listening to the voices in their heads. These students are communicating through their words and actions that they want to play a different game than the one they signed up for.

When the time comes for them to leave, the compassionate way is to mirror for them how *they chose to allow spiritual practice to fail them*. It wasn't the other way around.

They mustn't leave with the idea that the teachings or the community or the teacher didn't work or that they were unfairly treated. Sure, they might think that. The voices never like it when the sabotage they create doesn't get received the way it has always been received, either through people giving them their way or enabling their disturbance. Being a victim is a very popular way to get attention.

In spiritual practice, it's a little bit different. Getting what you want, expect, or feel you deserve isn't the point. The point is awakening. The methods required are whatever it will take – even if that means disappointing students.

Ultimately, the practice is compassionate enough to understand that even refusal of service and rejection can be a powerful teacher. In fact, it might be the event that kicks open a space for enlightenment!

BUDDHA SCHOOL DROPOUT

I never planned to train in a Zen monastery as a Zen monk for nearly 14 years. It's just something that happened.

It was something I continued to say "Yes" to every day until it was time to go.

After my first year, friends and family would ask, "Are you planning to stay there forever?"

My reply was something like, "I never planned to stay there at all. I'm there now. If I continue to stay there, I will be there. When I stop, I will stop being there. We'll see..."

The decision to leave the monastery was not easy. I had dedicated a good portion of my life to training there. I went from arriving as a fledgling monk who stuck signs on the porch furniture to someone who was entrusted to run multiple positions of responsibility in the organization.

I had major breakthroughs. And I had major breakdowns. It was an intense training, not to be found anywhere else on the planet, for which I am eternally grateful.

Several factors made it clear to me that it was time to move on.

About three-quarters of my way into my training, I had developed a cartoon series entitled "The Voices." Every Monday, the monastery published one of my cartoons to its email list. The list grew and the cartoon distribution expanded. I used the cartoon to bring humor and entertainment to the process of exposing the voices and how they caused us to struggle. People loved it.

Over time, my ideas for the cartoon evolved. I soon found myself making videos, creating songs, selling T-shirts, and promoting monastery events. One idea I had for a fundraiser featured a character in the cartoon. That fundraiser brought in well over $5,000. Another fundraiser was an auction to win one of ten handmade books I was making. That brought in $2,386. My practice, and my contribution to the practice, was at an all-time high.

My ultimate goal was to spread the teachings in a new way that was clear, accessible, light, and fun – words that didn't typically get associated with Zen.

As time went on, the focus of the monastery shifted. I was asked to do less with Sangha development. Monks were assigned more time tending the monastery's property, which was our retreat center. There were discussions about perhaps not producing new cartoons and instead republishing older ones. Our resources were tight and the monastery felt that we needed to prioritize the retreats we were offering.

I realized my creativity assisted my practice and the practice of others. I had different opinions about our priorities that led me to conclude it was time for me to say goodbye. I'm not going to suggest this was a clean break. I waffled back and forth about what to do. I had a beautiful dog under my direct care. The monastery was gorgeous and filled with the people I loved. Yet, resistance set in the longer I stayed. For the first part of my stay at the monastery, I used it as a shelter to hide from life. Now I wanted to give more, play bigger, and explode the practice to the world.

It became clear to me that the new lessons I needed to learn were going to come from living outside the monastery's gates.

Everything I was practicing with – communication, taking responsibility versus taking control, and ending my relationship with the voices – was going to happen in "the real world."

I gave away the belongings I didn't want to take with me. Every spare moment I had before leaving was spent with my dog. The only other time I had as much difficulty leaving was when I left my girlfriend at the bus station to go to the monastery thirteen and a half years ago.

My stomach was knotted. My throat had a lump.

Part of me was sad to leave, part of me was excited to start anew, part of me was terrified of what was to come, and all of me knew how to embrace those parts in conscious, compassionate awareness. To breathe and look forward. To take everything I had learned and to give back with the same coin I had been given.

It was a new day and a new time. I never planned to train and I never planned to leave. No one living in the present ever does.

STREAM OF CONSCIOUS
NOISE POLLUTION

People often ask me, "What is the hardest part about being out in the world since you left the monastery?" I have to say that it's social conversations.

I know this is going to sound horribly judgmental. In fact, I hesitate to say anything about it at all. However, I feel like I would be doing a grave disservice if I held back to be polite.

So here goes.

At the Zen monastery, we didn't engage in social conversations. At all.

In fact, here's the function of verbal communication in a monastic setting:

- Outside of group and guidance: To share information related to tasks with the head monk. Preferably via note; if necessary, in a whisper. To share work and retreat related details (only head monks and facilitators were involved in meetings).

- Inside of group and guidance: To process our insights from spiritual practice with the facilitator or guide.

We never sat around to talk or chat about anything.

Why? Because the monastery created and maintained a unique environment in which we could be left alone to have our own inner experiences while simultaneously being in community with others practicing the same. Everyone on the property was meditating every second of the day, either in formal sitting meditation, walking meditation, or working meditation. If you weren't doing a sitting or walking meditation, you were in working meditation, which included chopping carrots, cleaning the property, talking with retreatants, or walking back to your hermitage.

Social conversations didn't have a place at the monastery because they were the antithesis of our objective. The guidelines asked us not to look at what other people were doing, not to make eye contact, and not to talk to others.

Not because there's anything wrong with these activities; they just didn't have a place at the monastery.

Now that I'm out of the monastery, I can say truthfully that I have fallen in love with silence.

My headspace is such that I don't have the noisy jukebox going 24/7. I don't experience stress. I'm quite present to what is in front of me, and I am engaged with life. I enjoy being around others as much as I enjoy being alone with myself.

What I've noticed about social conversations, and why I learned not to miss them, is they mirror perfectly the voices in our heads.

The whole structure of social conversations reinforces our identities and solidifies our illusory "selves."

The next time you walk into a noisy bar or restaurant, see this dynamic for yourself: Groups of people engaged in what I call "stream of conscious noise pollution." Now please read "stream of conscious noise pollution" with a little tongue-in-cheek humor. I'm not suggesting that you allow the voices to judge others or yourself for engaging in social conversations. Not at all.

I'm attempting to bring consciousness to a potentially harmful habit that can reinforce the harmful habit in your mind.

Spiritual practice is, if nothing else, about embracing everything in conscious, compassionate awareness. The toughest part about social conversations is that it's so incredibly challenging to stay conscious, compassionate, and aware while you're in them. But it is possible.

How? Here are some of my favorite awareness tools:

1. Stay with your breath while you're in a conversation. Count your breath. It's easier to do this while you're listening than talking, but you can get better at it with practice.

2. Have a vibrating timer go off periodically as a reminder to check in with yourself. When it goes off, ask yourself, "Who's here?" "Am I still counting the breath?" "Am I choosing consciousness?"

3. Remain engaged with others. Don't allow your attention to wander around, ping-ponging all over the place (from your phone, to distractions, to the room, to your thoughts, etc.) Be active and deliberately present while staying aware of all.

4. Listen, and reflect back what others are saying. It will help you remain engaged because you won't be able to do it if you're not paying attention.

5. Hold something in your hand that will help ground you. I sometimes keep my index finger touching my thumb while I'm in public to keep my focus. If my finger and thumb aren't touching, or if I'm not holding my object, I'm not present.

6. Practice observing yourself, others, and the environment in silence. Expand your awareness to include as much as possible. Your Jedi skills will increase the more you stay *here* rather than in your head.

THE MOST NOTICEABLE,
VISIBLE DIFFERENCE

A t least once a year while I trained at the Zen monastery, the monks would load up all of our trucks and drive for hours to offer our New Year's retreat at a quaint villa by the ocean, run by the Sisters of Notre Dame. We would show up with chainsaws, weed-eaters, shovels, meditation cushions, and most of our kitchen.

Upon arriving, the appointed head monk would meet with the nun in charge. He or she would receive a list of projects from the villa that the sisters drafted.

In exchange for allowing us to put on a retreat at their lovely villa for free, we would do working meditation to prepare them for their upcoming retreat season. We would get a whole bunch of monks and a whole bunch of retreatants, and we would make magic happen there during the week. The list the sisters gave us included everything they wanted to have done right before opening the villa. It was a truly exhaustive list.

In the walk-through, the nun would let us know about the most important things on the list. She would point out what needed to be fixed, painted, and cleaned. She would also share some dream projects with us, things the sisters would never be able to do on their own but would love to see accomplished if it were possible.

After the tour, my teacher and our head monk would review the list and consider, "What would provide the villa with the most noticeable, visible difference?"

The sisters may have put a big star next to cleaning up the entire place. That would be very important in preparation for their guests coming after us. It would certainly get done and have some noticeable difference, for a little while anyway. However, building an entire fence between the church and the villa, or building a new raised garden bed behind the chapel, or painting a decorative sign over the private hermitage behind the villa – now *these* would be extremely noticeable! We would bump these "noticeable, visible difference" projects up to the very top of the list.

Why? Because at the end of the retreat there would be no denying it: Before there was no garden and now, *et voilà*, there is a garden!

The garden is a "noticeable, visible difference" the sisters will be talking about well after we leave. Visitors will remark on it. It'll be the one thing they remember when we ask to come again next year.

"Oh, those lovely Zen people showed up and built an entire raised garden bed area for us while they were here. What a joy it is to see the hummingbirds on the flowers and have fresh produce daily. How wonderful it would be to have them here again!"

I ask my clients, "What's the most noticeable, visible difference you and everyone around you will be raving about after our time together? What in your life would never have been there without us working together to create it? Let's put a star next to that and raise it to the top."

And now I'll ask you. How about you? What "noticeable, visible difference" would you like to create? What isn't in your life now, and what do you want there to be?

What would you, and others, be ogling over because of the noticeable, visible difference it's making in your life?

TO DO WHAT
YOU WERE MEANT TO DO

It can be very tempting to focus exclusively on: What I want for myself. What I want more of. What I want less of. How much I want to make. Who I want to become. How that affects my immediate sphere.

It can be very challenging to consider the world or the impact I want to make on others.

When I look inside, I see we are all similar. We're all well-meaning narcissists who live smack-dab at the center of our own universe. It's part of the human condition to see things from our narrow point of view. It's hard to expand and observe "the big cosmic scene."

It's also hard to describe the alternative. Sometimes I'm afraid I may sound like I'm saying people need to be utterly disinterested in themselves, as though I'm advocating a hard swing to one end of a selfless duality.

But that's not it. I want people to take care themselves, to care for the vehicle of their bodies, minds, and souls. To practice self-compassion and include themselves in the sphere of being worthy of their love and affection. Not better than, not less than, but rather part of the whole. Because they are.

I don't minimize accomplishments, big dreams or high aspirations. I want everyone to feel like they must be the very best they can be.

But there's also responsibility to the world.

Let's face it: The Universe doesn't care if you're happy or unhappy. It could care less about the emotional drama of your wants and desires. You're an insignificant speck, just like I am, and everyone else, too. *And* your magnanimous job here in this life is to evolve all of consciousness.

As much as you strive for it, your transformation doesn't end with your personal happiness. Nor your enlightenment. You don't get to retire to a mountain somewhere and *be* once you wake up. If you're going to awaken, you might as well go the whole distance and take the Bodhisattva vow, which is to save all sentient beings (and it's a pretty big job – there are lots of us). After waking up, the project becomes helping others across the same path you yourself have traversed.

In Zen's "Ten Bulls," once realization has happened, you go back out into the marketplace. It's one of the reasons I left the monastery where I trained. It was time to give back.

So yes, I want to strengthen myself. I want you to strengthen yourself. I want you to become radically successful. I want you to become a powerful force in the world.

Not just for yourself, but for everyone, because that's what it will take for you to have a magnificent impact in the world.

To do what you were meant to do.

NO BETTER IDEAS

I t all starts with a little voice. It sounds like a great idea at the time. "What's the harm, anyway?" the voice might say.

But when the investigation starts, and the teacher and the other monks are following the path of carnage to the origin, you'll see it all started with a little voice in some poor, unsuspecting monk's head.

I don't care how long that monk has been practicing. It's possible for the "better idea" beast to sneak in and take over at the slightest lapse in consciousness. It could be as innocuous as, "What's the harm in updating all of these recipes and removing the redundancy?" So when every recipe with beans starts with "Sort, rinse and soak beans," why not just remove the "sort, rinse and soak" part since that's a given? Seems logical. Saves space. Easier to read. Less typing.

Well, that's fine, if you know that sorting, rinsing and soaking beans is what you're supposed to do. But when the new head cook shows up on the scene, or the recipe is handed to a retreatant to follow, and months later a guest's tooth is broken on a rock found in the beans, all hell breaks loose.

The new head cook can do nothing but shrug her shoulders – she was just following the recipe. Then the recipes are revealed. Then they discover the recipes were changed. Then they search for the monk who changed them.

You may have guessed by now that I was the monk who removed "Sort, rinse, and soak beans" from every recipe with beans.

If you want to save yourself some trouble, master the art of catching the "better idea" beast.

In the beginning, focus on the scene of the crime. Breakdowns are a perfect place to start. Follow back over the sequence of steps that led to the mess. Ask, "How did this happen?" I bet you'll find that little voice that thought it would be a "better idea."

That's the voice you want to nail as soon as possible. That's the game you're playing – to catch sabotage in the making. To hear the voice making its case to remove "sort, rinse, and soak," to note the hesitation at the better idea, and to observe the voice that's insisting, "What's the harm?"

And to just say, "No."

MONKS WITH CHAINSAWS

One morning, my teacher and a couple other monks were preparing to leave the monastery to deliver a Zen workshop three hours away in the Bay Area. It had snowed the night prior, so we drove extra slowly around the narrow, winding road that led us off the property.

As we rounded the last bend, we were faced with an enormous evergreen that had fallen across the road, blocking our way out.

I recall my first thought was, "This must be a sign that we're not meant to do the workshop today."

To my amazement, the head monk whispered this very thought out loud to my teacher who sat in the back seat. After a brief chuckle, my teacher remarked, "Or it's a sign that we get out our chainsaws and cut our way through it!"

That's exactly what we did. All of us were highly trained to use chainsaws, including my teacher. After heading back to get them, we managed to clear away the tree and the branches enough to allow us safe passage through.

We drove out, delivered the workshop, and transformed lives that day.

I'll never forget how easily we projected meaning onto what we saw, believed it, and then assumed we should just give up.

How fortunate for us that we had our teacher there to model the art of getting present to a situation and then taking action based on what's appropriate, instead of believing the voices and assuming that "giving up" is the same thing as "letting go" or "Life's will."

A SIMPLE DESCRIPTION
OF THE SHIFT

When you're struggling, begin to uncover the voices in your head, voices that are operating behind the scenes.

Attempt to see the whole world through the lenses the voices provide for you. There's nothing more freeing than to objectively look at a reality you have been living in from the outside, and then to ultimately see the person in it (yourself) through the eyes of compassion.

To have an experience of this shift for yourself, please feel free to listen to my short, guided visualization, *Seeing Yourself Through the Eyes of Compassion* on my website: imagery.ashifttolove.com

CONSCIOUS COMPASSIONATE
COMMUNICATION

There you are with the back-and-forth dialog in your head, voices playing tennis with your mind, and you're caught in the middle. Dizzy, overwhelmed and confused. Lost with the voices that argue "Say this" or "Say that" or "Don't say that. Say *this*."

Meanwhile, the person you need to be talking with (the real person) hears nothing. Or worse, they hear partial information. Or inaccurate information. Or highly charged emotional information. Mental vomit instead of excellent communication. You've spent just a bit too long with the voices and now there's urgency instead of presence.

I always encourage good communication. One of the Eight Noble Truths from Buddhism is "Compassionate speech that makes for clarity."

Picture it: There's someone you need to be talking to, but instead, you're choosing to speak with the voices in your head. Does that strike you as odd too?

First, stop engaging with the illusions. It's a no-win relationship.

Next, determine with whom you'd like to have a conversation, a real person. Is it your partner? Your employee? Your child? Your coach? Your customer? Your Facebook friend? Who?

Then ask yourself, "Self, what do I have to communicate?"

These other questions can help you hone in on *how* to communicate:

- How can you share what you need to say from Center?
- How can you communicate from conscious, compassionate awareness?
- How can you use "I" statements to own your experience (instead of blame the other person)? Example: "When you do x, I feel y," (instead of "You're a y because you do x!").
- How can you practice reflective listening with the person?
- How can you clarify and draw out?
- How can you ask more gentle, curious questions?
- How can you listen again and say back what the person said?

Can you allow communication to become a dance instead of a war zone? A garden instead of a desert? A practice of presence instead of unconsciousness?

COMMITMENTS
AND SABOTAGE[†]

Commit to something (like working out) and pay attention to what happens. It doesn't matter what you commit to, whether it's meditating for five minutes upon waking, tidying up the house for 20 minutes per day, or sending a weekly email to someone that brightens their day.

Whatever it is, make an agreement with yourself to do it.

Next: Pay attention to how you do – or do not do – what you agreed to do. What do the voices say? Are they enthusiastic and excited, or are they resistant and complaining? Do they compare your success to others, or do they distract you from remembering your commitment entirely so that you "forget?"

Or something else?

Pay attention to all of it. Be a super sleuth.

If you get derailed, simply recommit. Don't buy into the voices' assessments of you.

Drop them and jump into the game again.

See how they throw you back into the pot.

Get out.

Fall back into the pot.

Get out.

See everything you can about the process.

Awareness is key.

Commit only to see and learn everything you can about how you do, or not do, everything.

FEAR OF FEELING

People are at war with their feelings. They are so afraid of how they felt in the past or what they will feel in the future that they box themselves up and twist themselves up into knots for fear of feeling the "wrong" way. Ironically, they make themselves feel worse than before in the process.

With all the information we have today about positive and spiritual psychology, I've talked to people who have become more self-conscious rather than free. They say they are trying not to judge or compare. When they do, they "beat themselves up" for judging and comparing.

Now, this is utterly silly.

We judge and compare all the time. Human beings have the natural capacity to experience ourselves as separate, which gives us the ability to experience suffering as well as compassion. Unconsciousness as well as consciousness. Hell as well as bliss.

As with anything in the practice I teach, it isn't *what* you feel or do. It's *how* you feel or do.

For example, "judgment" from conscious, compassionate awareness is what I call "discernment." If I hear the voices in my head judging someone or something else, I can use that to see how those voices cause me to suffer. This is incredibly helpful. Why would I want to stop? Judgment in this way can help me understand how *I* need to help *myself* become different. It becomes a pathway to transformation.

The same is true with comparison. President Theodore Roosevelt once said "Comparison is the thief of joy." No, it's not! The voices in our heads are the thieves of joy. Comparison can help motivate me to close the gap between where I am now and where I want to be. It could inform what I need to learn. It could help me get present to habitual states of mind so I can drop them and choose presence.

My teacher would walk into a room and start talking, and I would be in awe of her big thinking. The voices would immediately try to make me feel bad about how I'm not like her, but consciously I knew I could use her modeling to inform what living, breathing, big-thinking looked like. It inspired me to step out of my limited thinking.

Feelings are our opportunity to look beyond conditioned assumptions. What if they don't mean what we've been taught they mean? What if striving for one over another is futile?

In my experience, presence and peace aren't a matter of flicking some internal switch and achieving "flatline." That's death. Presence and peace are riding the waves and soaking in the sunshine. Both. Without meanings, emotions can be our gateway to freedom instead of suffering.

Worth an experiment!

THE DEADLY PAUSE

So then because thou art lukewarm, and neither cold nor hot, I will spue thee out of my mouth.
—*Jesus Christ*

If you need to think about it, you're not ready. The answer is "no."

I have learned, through my own experience, that if my eyes roll up into thought and I'm pausing, my choice has already been made for me.

You see, commitment is big.

When I found Zen and realized my life was starting to become better because it was in my life, I didn't "wonder if I was going to go meditate," and I didn't "hope to end up at a monastery," and I didn't "guess I was going to train deeper." Every fiber of my being screamed "*Yes!*" And I began to take the necessary steps required to get me from where I was to where I needed to be.

Only the heart can make such choices, because the heart operates in decisionless decisions.

The head needs to weigh out options. It needs to measure the pluses and the minuses. It needs to see if the R.O.I. is significant enough and if there isn't something better out there to consider first. It needs to put things off indefinitely because this decision is so serious.

What I will tell you is the voices would *love* to shelve your life into "maybe/someday," so on a day when there's no going back, the voices will gut you with regret. They'll paint a beautiful life you wasted on "playing small and being safe," dangle it in front of your face, and then light it on fire while you weep.

Until then, my recommendation is to check in with your heart. When presented with an opportunity, ask yourself if it has the potential to open you up to limitless possibilities. Your heart knows.

Check in to see how much fear is present. Use it to inform you instead of scare you. Because on the other side of every great fear is a proportionally great joy waiting for you to leap.

Remember.

If you hesitate too long, you will miss. The portal will close, and the party will move on to the next town.

Only now is real.

Use it.

T hink about yourself for just a moment.

How would you describe yourself?

When you meet people, what do you typically tell them?

Do you start your chat by telling them what you do for a living? Do you mention your relationship status? Do you share your favorite recreational activities?

If you were to talk longer to get to know them, what else would you say? How much deeper would you go?

How about with your friends, and the people whom you have known the longest? How would you describe yourself to these people?

Now imagine for a moment that you're alone in a room.

Just you, by yourself.

Start filling in the blanks about what you know about yourself, things that no one else could possibly know. Begin to collect all of your traits and characteristics, adjectives and roles, identities and personas.

Imagine that I'm there in the room with you to the side, adding what you're discovering to a giant whiteboard. I'm scribing neatly at first, with columns and rows. But soon I'm adding words and phrases into any available space I can find. I'm creating half-rows and half-columns with smaller and smaller writing. Notice me running out of room quickly!

There's your name, your bad habits, your saving graces, your social security number, your embarrassing secrets, your proud moments, your friends, your talents, your obsessions, your fears, your insecurities, your job title, your preferred foods, your hobbies, your enemies, your favorite books, your awards, your enthusiasm for "these activities" and your dislike for "those activities"...

They're all you!

Or are they?

Maybe some of those things are what you decided to believe, despite all provable evidence to the contrary. Perhaps you've held onto an idea of yourself since kindergarten when someone said something about you. Maybe you were given this identity against your will when you went for that diagnosis. Perhaps you know others who are a certain way *more* than you are (and certainly *less* than you, too). Maybe you got so accustomed to these ways of being and so comfortable with them and received so much attention for them that you didn't bother looking any further for something different.

Are you panicking a little right now as I take a big ol' whiteboard eraser to this jumbled up, tangled up mess that's "you" and wipe the board clean?

Are you screaming, "No! *Stop!* That's *me!*"?

As the last few remnants of black ink vanish and the whiteboard space regains dominance again, perhaps you're relaxing a little. Maybe your shoulders have dropped and fallen back. Or your jaw has gotten less clenched. The tightness in your gut has released.

Maybe you're breathing a tiny bit easier now seeing *nothing* on the board.

"Ahhhh... "

Maybe the clean, open space is the *truth* about you. The truth that nothing was ever nailed down, solid, permanent, real, indelible, fixed or forever about you. That the only *real truth* right now is what you can see in front of you.

The view before you.

The step you can take directly ahead of you.

That opens up to the next view.

More steps. More views.

Infinite possibilities. No boundaries. No history.

Nothingness.

From this nothingness, everything arises.

That's what it's like when there is no "you" in the way.

HOW BREATHTAKING!†

We were in a narrow little space off the monastery's main building called the Work Director's Office. The one thing that saved it from being a simple closet was the enormous window that spanned the entire length of the wall. From this window, you could see an expanse of forest.

My teacher, another senior monk and I were having a quick business meeting late that afternoon in the Work Director's Office. We wanted to address some monastery issues and get guidance on them.

The other monk and I were quickly making our cases for what was most important. We went back and forth with our arguments. Both of us hoped our teacher would see the wisdom and logic in our presentation and choose our suggested course of action.

Suddenly, in the middle of our debate, she gasped, "How breathtaking!"

I looked up at the other monk who stood across from me. I was able to catch her incredulous expression that likely mirrored my own. For all I know, I may have even sighed in annoyance.

We both looked at our teacher's face. Her eyes were wide in amazement. So, we followed her gaze out the window to see what caught her attention.

The light streaming through the trees was indeed breathtaking. We lived on over 380 acres of stunning forest in the foothills. You couldn't take a step anywhere on the property without some natural beauty stopping you in your tracks.

Immediately everything that seemed so important – "my view versus my opponent's view" – dissolved.

In my head, I could hear the voices screaming at my teacher for interrupting us.

"How irresponsible. Hasn't she seen views like this before? Why now? This is so disruptive. Now we'll be off topic. Can't she pay attention? Must she be so distracted? She's a Zen teacher for crying out loud!"

But I got it. I knew that she just helped us both disidentify from the grip egocentricity had on us. I could tell by the resistant energy arising in me that she broke through and got us to the other side – to the present.

When the voices have us, and our worldview is small and limited, it's time to drop it. There's a bigger picture here, and it's waiting for us to see it: Life is magnificent, and we can choose to exist in the present.

When we're in the present, we can then consciously resume our business. We can continue with a clearer head, a more extensive worldview, less urgency, and room for exhilarating insights, which includes breathtaking views!

SUPPORT THAT
WHICH SUPPORTS YOU

Every so often, the Zen monastery sent out emails to the Sangha to share the monastery's financial situation with the community. It was usually a report to say that expenses have gone up but not donations. This would produce a flurry of income to keep the monastery's doors open for the time being.

Since the beginning, my teacher was adamant that people would experience the value of the work and give to keep it alive or they wouldn't. She wasn't going to sell the teachings, so it was up to all of us to do our part. She was happy for it to go either way. I loved her attitude of "it'll work, or it was a grand experiment that failed."

Now that I've been out of the monastery, I have been involved in hosting personal development events both large and small. I've seen the amount of work that goes into planning them, marketing them, executing them and following up with them.

I co-hosted one event a couple of times with my partner and a colleague. The first time we offered it, the weekend was a huge success and incredibly rewarding. People flew in from all over the world to participate and we received numerous "thank-yous" for making it possible for them to attend. Stories came out months later that the weekend was a turning point for several of the attendee's careers and personal lives.

The second time around, we noticed the general attitude about registering was ambivalent. We heard, "I'll register next year." "Funds are low now," or "I have other plans," or "I've done too many personal development events this year already." "Next year..."

Until we decided that there wasn't going to be a "next year."

We didn't offer the event again. We didn't get enough interest.

The moral of the story is: If you value something, support it.

Look around you right now, in your own home and in the whole world. What are you putting there? What are you helping to flourish?

Either you choose compassion, or you choose suffering. Humanity either works, or it's a grand experiment that failed.

It's really up to you. The responsibility is yours.

There's no need to experience overwhelm about it. No need for the voices to use this as one more thing to feel bad about.

Pick something. Anything. No matter how small. Support it. Give it your love and attention. A flower will bloom more beautifully with your care. A child will open up with your listening. A grandparent will do better with your hand.

Say "thank you" to that which supports you. Support what supports you in whatever way you can.

Allow love to continue.

RIPPING THE SKIN OFF THE SNAKE[†]

here are two ways:

      The violent, painful, cruel and pointless way.

      Or the natural, timely and gentle way.

The snake's skin will be shed the moment it needs to be and no sooner.

At the right time.

We get impatient and rip ourselves apart in our race to success, happiness, and fulfillment.

How can we slow down and move with life and its cues? To follow the path and see the main view when we arrive at the main view? Trusting that the main view does not show up earlier but rather when we arrive?

Everything in its due time.

ne person; two possibilities.

1. "I'm broken, and I need to heal. I've got problems I need to fix and a past I need to overcome."
2. "I'm perfect, yet I want to grow. I've got projects I want to work on and an exciting future to create."

What lenses do you see yourself and life through?

PLEASE TAKE THE TIME†

Nobody sees a flower really; it is so small. We haven't time, and to see takes time - like to have a friend takes time.
—*Georgia O'Keeffe*

If you hear yourself say you don't have time for what you know will take good care of you – like meditation, like being healthy, like practicing kindness – then please stop...

...and take care of yourself.

Please take the time.

Don't miss the "small" things here for an imaginary future out there.

The voices would like to speed you along straight to your death.

Refuse to follow along. They are not your friends.

Take the time.

Create the time.

Never feel bad again. For anything.

A beating never makes you into a better person – only a fearful one afraid of doing something wrong.

Imagine learning from your "mistakes" as a way to grow and become better. When life isn't going your way, it is not a sign that you need to give up. In fact, setbacks are springboards to possibilities.

Nothing that happens *means* anything.

Imagine having someone help you learn by reviewing events that happened in the past with compassion, patience, and acceptance. Together, you can come up with the support you need to overcome your challenges and accomplish your dreams in the future.

Let's face it, it's much more inspirational to take on the impossible than to "fix how you are broken." Every child knows this, yet we live with an inner critic and a head-banging noise machine that makes escape from ourselves the ultimate goal. We cannot sit in silence or be alone with ourselves for any length of time because there is nothing to reflect the ego anywhere.

We hate ourselves and expect to find love "out there."

Consider this...

...the state of the world is a mirror for the state of our minds.

Are you ready for a new mind and a new world? It starts when we take responsibility for ourselves. When we learn and practice a new way.

It starts when we change our relationship with ourselves: From lost in thought to present, conscious, and aware.

ACKNOWLEDGMENTS
AND GRATITUDE

Gratitude is a conscious practice. It's not done on autopilot. In my workshops, I joke about how no one spontaneously, accidentally breaks out into gratitude lists. It's far easier to allow the mind to stumble off into what's wrong, what could be different, or what more is needed. To express gratitude takes effort, deliberateness, and presence.

So here goes!

I would like to thank my life partner, Karen Davis, for her endless love and patience with me. She may call me her "conscious man," but after spending 14 years in a Zen monastery, it doesn't make me someone easy to live with (think Mork and Mindy). She is my biggest cheerleader who supports me with endless encouragement.

Thank you to my fans, readers, clients, students and workshop participants. My interactions with you have transformed my life and keep the practice alive within my heart now that I no longer live at the monastery. You require me to show up and I require you to show up when the voices say, "You don't want to."

Deep Gasshō to the Zen monastery, the monks, my teacher, Sangha, the teachings and all those who came before us to make this wonderful practice available. The world so desperately needs it, you and us.

Thank you to Mom, Dad, and Andy for being my family. I appreciate you always being there for me no matter how weird my life decisions appear to be.

Thank you to my amazing book editor, Sara Stibitz. She puzzle-pieced these stories and lessons together and polished them brightly with love and care.

And thanks to Jax, our furry, four-legged Zen Master who so diligently trains me every day.

ABOUT THE AUTHOR

Alex Mill is a Zen Life and Leadership Coach. He trained in a Zen monastery for nearly 14 years and now offers his extensive experience to help people transform their lives and businesses from the inside-out through mindfulness, meditation, and compassionate self-mentoring practices. He is the creator of the life-changing, 30-day online retreats, *Heart-to-Heart: Compassionate Self-Mentoring* and its sequel, *Help Yourself to Change*. He offers an online version of his Zen meditation workshop entitled, *Taming Your Inner Noise*, where you can learn how to meditate and experience why meditation is so important. He is the author of three other books on Zen awareness practice: *Practicing Presence, Meditation and Reinventing Yourself,* and *The Zen Life: Spiritual Training for Modern Times*.

If you'd like to learn more about Zen Life Coaching, please go to his website, coaching.zenlife.coach, and send an email requesting more information. You will receive a beautiful 30-page booklet outlining *What You Need to Know Before Hiring a Coach*.

Alex lives in Louisville, Colorado with his partner in compassionate transformation, Karen Davis, and their English Crème Retriever, the aggressive cuddler, Prince Jax, Master of All He Surveys (Jax for short).

You can read more about Alex's books, retreats, workshops and latest offerings at www.zenlife.coach.

WHAT NOW?

"How do you direct your attention to the present moment?"

"How do you keep your focus on being the compassionate Inner Mentor?"

This book, and all of my written works, is in service to opening up a new way of seeing. To create a shift. It's like a doorway with a view. Sometimes the view is heart opening, sometimes it's breathtaking, and at other times it's provocative. But all of the views attempt to show you what's possible when you're present and what happens when you're not.

Like anything else, "the how" is in the experience. Just like you wouldn't be able to learn how to ride a bicycle from reading a book, you wouldn't be able to learn how to direct your attention consciously or be the compassionate Inner Mentor from reading a book, either. That comes from you taking action and experiencing these ways of being for yourself, and then practicing them.

Since I left the monastery, I have created a few programs that were designed to assist with "the how." It's where most of my time and labor-of-love have gone. I want people all over the world to experience the deep transformational work I experienced in my Zen training – without needing to travel to some remote monastery to have it.

First, I highly recommend Zen meditation. There are hundreds of different types of meditation practices, from putting on headphones and listening to binaural beats, to lying down and leaving your body, to focusing on a mantra or a candle flame, to chanting and ringing gongs, to body scanning, to jogging, etc. So, when people say they "meditate," I want to be clear that we are definitely *not* talking about the same thing.

Zen meditation (Zazen) trains your attention to stay in the present moment. It's a practical tool designed to facilitate you becoming awake, relaxed, and alert, and not just while you're in formal sitting meditation. It was designed to help you be present in your day-to-day life. Unlike many other meditation practices, it's not some special experience you do and...that's it. It's not entertainment. It's more like going to the gym to have a workout. Sometimes it's fun and other times it's gruesome. You're not required to "enjoy" it. It's something you do to help yourself maintain health and fitness. The same is true with Zen meditation and awareness practice.

The program I created to teach you how to meditate is my online Zen meditation workshop called "Taming Your Inner Noise." This online workshop is an on-demand video training that not only teaches you *how* to meditate, but it also shows you why you want to start meditating right now, what you'll run into as you continue, and how to set up a home practice. Plus, I provide ongoing support in the form of Motivational Meditation Emails and a physical copy of my book, *Meditation and Reinventing Yourself*. You can register for this online, on-demand workshop anytime: www.tamingyourinnernoise.com.

To help you keep your attention on compassion and be your authentic self, I highly recommend "Heart-to-Heart: Compassionate Self-Mentoring." This 30-day online retreat will expose the voices in your head and show you how to create a relationship with the wise, loving, compassionate part of yourself who can guide your life perfectly. Grads have told me they left this retreat empowered, confident, clear, and in-tune with their creative, compassionate wisdom. Please feel free to read the 40+ testimonials on my site if you want to hear what they had to say about it: www.compassionretreat.com.

One more piece of information that isn't public yet: There is a follow-up retreat after "Heart-to-Heart: Compassionate Self-Mentoring." It's called "Help Yourself to Change," and it gives you the opportunity to take the work you started even deeper. For the longest time, grads were asking me if I could please create a "part two" course that would support their practice. I'm happy to say this retreat now exists. Based on the feedback I've been given, it sounds like it's delivering on the promise of being an advanced course full of eye-opening experiences. There is no link to share with you about this retreat because it's not available to the public. It's an invitation-only retreat for select grads of "Heart-to-Heart: Compassionate Self-Mentoring." The reason I mention it here is because I want you to know that if you're serious about taking the awareness practice I shared in this book as far as you can, there are opportunities for you to do so.

I show up for those who show up, but it's going to be 100% up to you.

Lastly, I also coach clients from all over the world. My availability is extremely limited and I typically invite only the most committed, willing, open-minded people who are not afraid of change. If that's you, please contact me through my website: coaching.zenlife.coach

I hope this clarifies a little bit about how you can get "the how" of what I wrote here in this book. I learned first-hand that the books I was reading were simply showing me what's possible. I had to sit down and meditate and then train in a monastery before anything significant happened.

Practice is called practice for a reason. It's definitely not a spectator sport.

If you have any questions about these offerings, please feel free to reach out to me. I'd be happy to answer them.

In lovingkindness,

Alex

BOOKS BY ALEX MILL

- Practicing Presence

- Meditation and Reinventing Yourself

- The Zen Life: Spiritual Training for Modern Times

PROGRAMS BY ALEX MILL

- Taming Your Inner Noise: A Zen Meditation Workshop

- Heart-to-Heart: Compassionate Self-Mentoring

- Help Yourself to Change

Made in the USA
Columbia, SC
09 December 2018